D0343327

LOSING MEGAN

FINDING HOPE, COMFORT AND FORGIVENESS IN THE MIDST OF MURDER

TOM KOHL

WESTBOW
PRESS
A DIVISION OF THOMAS NELSON

WestBow Press books may be ordered through booksellers or by contacting:

WestBow Press
A Division of Thomas Nelson
1663 Liberty Drive
Bloomington, IN 47403
www.westbowpress.com
1-(866) 928-1240

Because of the dynamic nature of the Internet, any web addresses or links contained in this book may have changed since publication and may no longer be valid. The views expressed in this work are solely those of the author and do not necessarily reflect the views of the publisher, and the publisher hereby disclaims any responsibility for them.

Any people depicted in stock imagery provided by Thinkstock are models, and such images are being used for illustrative purposes only.

Certain stock imagery © Thinkstock.

ISBN: 978-1-4497-7637-4 (sc)
ISBN: 978-1-4497-7638-1 (e)

Library of Congress Control Number: 2012921480

All Photographs by Megan's mother, Teresa Flynn Kohl

Printed in the United States of America

WestBow Press rev. date: 01/04/2013

CONTENTS

PREFACE

I began writing this book on July 21, 2010. This was the fourth anniversary of my daughter's murder.

Megan was born on May 31, 1985, and she died on July 21, 2006. She was brutally murdered by someone she considered a friend.

This is the story of my daughter's addiction to drugs and the drug court I helped establish. And it's the story of how the two merged together to forge a ministry of hope, comfort and forgiveness in a county courthouse.

In July of 2010 I was driving in my car to work out at the gym. I was listening to a radio program on a local Christian station. The host was talking to a pastor from the East coast who had just published a book about the death of his young son by suicide. The topic caught my interest.

When I arrived at the gym, I sat in my car in the parking lot, listening to the interview. Later that day I contacted the station to get some information about the pastor. I called him within the week and we talked for an hour. I told him about Megan and he told me about his son. I asked him about the process of writing a book. I was pumped and I began to pray to God about what He wanted me to do. Within a few days, God answered that prayer.

This story reveals how God can work through the most horrific set of circumstances bringing hope to those who are desperate, hope to those who are lost, hope to those who are suffering and even hope in the midst of murder.

Romans 8:28 says:

"And we know that in all things God works for the good of those who love him, who have been called according to his purpose."

Jesus is in the business of saving, forgiving and comforting. This book shows how He did this in my life.

I became a judge in May of 1997, was the Presiding Judge from 2006 through 2010. I am currently a sitting judge in Washington County, Oregon. I have refused to talk to the media about Megan's death. I have not watched local television news since July 21, 2006. I am now ready to share this walk with whoever wants to come along.

DEDICATION

To Megan, Zac, Julie and my granddaughter, Vienne, who went to spend eternity with Jesus on September 6, 2012.

No parent should ever have to see

the death certificate

of their child.

NEVER

CHAPTER 1
PRISON VISIT

On April 21, 2011, five of my closest buddies sat in the Suburban outside the Umatilla prison. As the guards processed me through the myriad of security checkpoints, I knew those guys were praying. And that's exactly why I brought them.

I was ushered through thick steel doors, deeper into the confines of the quiet prison. With each ominous creak and heavy-handed slam, I felt the blood rush faster through my veins. My comfort level quickly began to fall.

Was I really prepared for this?

Even though I had been a judge for more than thirteen years, I had never once stepped foot inside a prison. I had no need. My work was in the courtroom. Yet the last four years had taken me on a much different, darker path. This was the natural progression of what seemed to be an inevitable course. And the fact was...this is exactly what I had asked for.

I had no agenda. No real questions. In all honesty, I didn't really know what I was looking for. Yet it was clear God had put it on my heart. Nearly four months ago I had requested a meeting, and within a week, I had the response in my hand, complete with a visitor's application and affirmation to meet.

The process would prove more difficult than first anticipated. Victims, as they called people like me, were not allowed to meet with inmates. Protocol had to be met. Counseling sessions had to take place. And the biggest hurdle of all...inmates had to acknowledge responsibility for their crime. Given the fact that Robert was in the middle of the appeal process, I never thought he would admit his guilt. Yet, a few phone calls and several prayers later, I had the answer I wanted.

The door locked behind me, and my skin crawled. The smell of institutional cleaning chemicals was in the air. Nothing could have prepared me for this. I desperately needed God's presence.

When the door opened across from me, Robert, clad in prison garb, walked into the small conference room.

It was the man who had brutally murdered my daughter.

CHAPTER 2
THE KNOCK ON THE DOOR

July 21, 2006. 11pm. The knock on the front door, followed by the ringing of the doorbell, startled my wife Julie and I from our sleep. Reluctantly I put on some sweats and a T-shirt and went downstairs to find out who could be knocking on our door so late at night.

When I reached the bottom of the steps, through the front door window the porch light revealed a familiar face, Roger Hanlon, the Chief Deputy with the Washington County District Attorney's office.

As a judge I knew Roger well because he had appeared in front of me on numerous occasions. When Roger was in my courtroom for a case it was a serious matter, like robbery or assault or murder. The two other people were strangers, a man and a woman whom I didn't recognize.

Usually, when police come to my home, there is a courtesy phone call first to see if I am available to review and sign a search warrant for them. A half hour later, I review the warrant, sign it and off they go to serve it on some unsuspecting drug dealer or other potential criminal.

A major crime must have been committed if they didn't call first.

I invited Roger and the two strangers into my living room, and I waited for them to tell me about the search warrant.

The man on Roger's right introduced himself as Detective Luke Streight with the Milwaukie, Oregon Police Department. The woman with him worked for the victims' assistance program in the Clackamas County District Attorney's office.

Detective Streight didn't make small talk. He said, "Judge, Megan is dead."

I couldn't believe it.

This was not happening.

Again, he said, "Megan is dead."

To hear someone say, "Your child is dead" is the most devastating phrase imaginable. It felt like someone had just kicked me in the gut. Visions of her lifeless body overwhelmed me, and I cried out in utter horror at the thought of never being able to see my daughter again. Sobbing uncontrollably, I thought *how could my Heavenly Father allow this to happen?* A parent's worst nightmare had just begun.

Julie heard my cries from our bedroom upstairs and came rushing down the steps to see what was happening. I told her that Megan was dead.

Time stood still as we retreated into our kitchen to be alone, embrace and cry together. We clung to each other tightly for minutes…hours. I don't know how long we cried together before we came back into the living room where Roger, the detective and the victims' assistance person were still seated.

The detective went on to explain that Megan had been murdered in an apartment complex in Gladstone where she had been staying with some friends. Her body was found earlier that day at approximately 4pm, inside the apartment on the kitchen floor. The detective wouldn't say how Megan was murdered, just that it was extremely violent.

Megan was dead.

The investigation had begun.

Someone had taken my daughter's life, but we wouldn't know who killed her until June 1, 2007, almost a year later.

CHAPTER 3
A CHILD IS BORN

It was May 31,1985. The air was warm. The sun bright. As any young father, my heart pounded with pride and my mind raced with questions...

Would I be good enough to be her dad?

Could I protect her? Provide for her?

Could I keep her from the evil in this world?

Megan was born on May 31, 1985, at St. Vincent Hospital in Portland. A few blocks from our home. We knew we were going to have a little girl by the ultrasound which occurred a few months before her birth.

Her mother and I settled on her name with little controversy. The birth certificate announced her arrival at 2:11pm as Meghan Flynn Kohl. The spelling of her name would morph and grow along with its owner. From "Meghan" to "Meaghan" to "Meagan" and then to "Megan," the way she will always be remembered by my pen. Simple. Straightforward. Beautiful.

She was a precious child. Perfect in every way. Friends told us that Megan looked like a little China doll in those early days. Fair

6

skinned, rosy cheeks. Big, beautiful blue eyes. The epitome of beauty. My joy.

Megan was not your typical little girl; she was a tomboy through and through. She loved to play in the mud and go fishing. She played soccer, softball and basketball. I had the privilege of being her coach in many of her sports activities. One summer she played on a competitive girls' softball team. Her team had over sixty games that summer. I didn't miss one! I was so proud of her.

She was a caring and compassionate child, generous and kind to her childhood friends. She loved animals, cats and horses, especially.

She was also a very strong-willed child. Her mother, Teresa, used to struggle to no end trying to get her dressed for school in the mornings. Megan would not compromise. If she wasn't ready to get dressed, she wouldn't. If Megan didn't want to do something, she didn't.

During Megan's elementary school years she would often come running to greet me when I arrived home from work. Grabbing one of my legs, she would shout "Daddy, Daddy, I love you!"

I will never forget those precious moments.

Our first child, Zachary, was born on July 19, 1983, also at St. Vincent Hospital. As a child, Zac had little interest in his sister. He was more interested in his collection of plastic dinosaurs, reptiles and fish.

As the kids grew older, Zac would become one of her best friends and a protector. But when they were children, Zac and Megan would get into the typical sibling arguments. Sometimes I would come into the room as they were arguing. Megan, crying that Zac had hit her, would convince me that he was at fault. A father's heart for his daughter sometimes overlooked the obvious and Zac would get the discipline. Poor Zac. I think Zac has forgiven me. At times Megan would get mad at me for disciplining Zac when I "believed" her version of the story!

As a family, we attended a local Catholic church. There were some years that we attended more often than others. We heard the name of Jesus every time we went although I didn't have a personal relationship with Him until much later in my life.

Megan was baptized and confirmed in that church. She received her first communion in that church. Her funeral was in that church.

I remember tucking her in bed at night when she was a toddler. I looked forward to those moments, those sweet memories of time spent with Megan. Often I would pray that prayer with her that we all remember as children:

Now I lay me down to sleep,
I pray the Lord, my soul to keep,
If I should die before I wake,
I pray the Lord, my soul to take.

And then together we would say, "Amen!" and I would quietly leave her bedroom when she fell asleep. I never really believed that the Lord would take her home, at least not before he took me.

The days and weeks shortly after her death, I would pray that same prayer again and again in my mind. And I always remembered my little girl, folding her hands and asking God to take her soul.

Chapter 4
Panic in the Night

In the early to mid-ninety's our family vacations were spent in Sunriver, Oregon. Sunriver is a private resort located in the high desert area of central Oregon. The area boasts of having sunshine over three hundred days a year as compared to the Portland area where the sun is seldom seen except in the summer time.

Sunriver has over sixty miles of bike trails, swimming pools, tennis courts, a small shopping area, two world class golf courses and plenty of fishing holes nearby. Sunriver also has horse stables for its residents and guests. Megan was a horse fanatic. Her mother, Teresa, grew up with a profound love for horses and this was passed down to Megan.

I remember one summer vacation at Sunriver when Megan was allowed to "work" at the stables. She helped feed the horses, clean the stalls and lead the ponies around the ring while other little children rode them.

Megan and I got up at 5am each morning so I could get her to the stables in time to feed and clean. She would work for hours and she loved it. Her reward was a two-hour horse ride at the end of the day in the BLM lands surrounding Sunriver.

Another time in Sunriver we had some friends over for a barbecue. There was an awesome storm that evening, and we lost power. It never rained, but there were lightning strikes everywhere. It looked like a Fourth of July celebration.

After our friends left, we noticed that Megan was nowhere in sight. It was dark and we started to call for her. There was no answer. We began searching the two story house. We searched all the rooms including her bedroom. Megan was nowhere to be found. All my fears about being a good father and being able to protect her were racing through my mind. Had I failed her now?

We began to panic, shouting her name.

No answer.

As I searched outside the house, I remembered that Megan had been in the hot tub earlier that night. I ran back to the hot tub and frantically yanked the cover off.

Megan was not there.

Relief for the moment and then panic again, although this time the panic was more intense.

Then I heard the most wonderful words from her mom, "Megan is here...she's in her bedroom!"

Her mom had discovered her on the floor between the bed and the wall...sleeping!

I knew at that moment in time how precious each minute is with our children. That night, I'd glimpsed into the darkness, the anguish at what it was like to lose my child. I did not want to ever experience that again. My efforts to provide and protect were doubled, tripled.

CHAPTER 5
ZAC'S TWENTY-THIRD
BIRTHDAY

On July 19, 2006, Zac and I were getting together for dinner that evening to celebrate his twenty-third birthday.

Zac was born almost two years before Megan, and he became a fisherman at the age of about three when he caught his first rainbow trout at Battleground Lake in southwestern Washington State. He was hooked on fishing for the next twelve years. Zac wanted to go fishing, any time, any place. When it was time to go home, a battle would usually ensue. Zac did not want to leave. Oftentimes in tears, Zac would have to be carried back to the truck, a very unhappy boy.

Zac became an excellent fly fisherman, learning to tie his own flies at the young age of ten. He was one of the best little fisherman on any lake or stream wherever he happened to be fishing. He preferred to catch and release, not wanting to harm any of his quarry. There were days at Sunriver he would fish for up to eight hours at a time.

Zac grew up to be 6'3" and is one of the most handsome young men I have ever seen (I realize I'm biased but...) Dedicated to his passion, Zac went on to "wrestle bigger fish" studying the circulatory system of alligators as his thesis for his PhD in Biology.

In the fall of 1999, the kids' mom and I separated. After our divorce became final in October of 2000, my relationship with my kids was estranged. The fact that children of divorce suffer the most is a given. It is not part of God's plan to see a marriage end in divorce. I had not yet accepted Christ as my Lord and Savior. I did not know Jesus nor the power and difference He can make in a marriage. It is not an excuse; it is just a fact.

I worked hard on reestablishing my relationship with Zac and Megan. Zac was open to reconciliation and restoration. Megan was not.

So back to July 19, 2006.

Zac had taken the light rail train, called MAX, from southeast Portland to Hillsboro, about twenty miles. He had just moved into a new apartment with a friend from college. This apartment was in an area that I was not familiar with, so we agreed to meet at Quatama station in Hillsboro.

Zac rode his bike from his apartment to the closest light rail station in Portland. When he arrived at Quatama, we had to disassemble his front wheel so I could put the bike in the back of my 4-runner.

I asked Zac where he would like to go for his birthday dinner. He said he was hungry for Indian food, so I decided on a local Indian restaurant in the Orenco Station area of Hillsboro.

It had been almost seven years since his mom and I had divorced. I was working hard to be the father that God wanted me to be, but it was difficult. I became anxious and nervous whenever Zac and I got together. Praying helped, but I was struggling with the guilt of a father who failed his children and their mother. Though I had asked for their forgiveness I still tended to struggle with that.

"The Lord is compassionate, merciful, patient and always ready to forgive." Psalm 103:9 God's Word

Thankfully, even though I still struggled, I knew that my Father in Heaven had completely and totally forgiven me for my past failures.

When we arrived at the parking lot, Zac and I got out of the truck and started walking to the restaurant. Zac turned to me with this quizzical look on his face and said, "Dad, are you going to turn the engine off?" I looked back and realized that I had left the keys in the ignition with the engine running!

Zac had a big grin on his face. I sheepishly went back to the truck, turned the engine off and pulled the key from the ignition.

With my truck safely turned off, we went into the restaurant and had a wonderful meal and enjoyable time with each other. This was Zac's twenty-third birthday. I drove him back to his new apartment in Southeast Portland after dinner. This was my first visit to his new place.

My relationship with Zac was vastly improving. I knew God had forgiven me. I sensed that Zac was starting to experience that same forgiveness also. I was desperately praying that Megan would do the same.

Two days later there was a knock on our door.

CHAPTER 6
TELLING ZAC

The night of Megan's murder, the detective told Julie and I that the major crimes team in Clackamas County was called in to investigate the murder. He would not give us any additional information. The victims' assistance person gave us her card with all the pertinent information on it. We could tell that this was going to take some time. We did not realize how much time.

Zac and his mother, had yet to be told. Roger asked me if he could drive me over to Zac's place because I was in no condition to drive. I did not want to deliver this horrible news to Zac over the phone, so I accepted Roger's offer.

As we were getting into his car, Roger asked me where Zac lived. It struck me then that I had only been to Zac's new apartment once before on his birthday two days earlier. And it had been at night.

While driving Zac back to his apartment on the 19th of July, I wasn't even paying attention to how we got there. I was just following his directions, "Turn right here, Dad, go to the next stop light and turn left..."

I told Roger that I didn't know exactly where Zac lived, but I knew the general area. I quietly wept as we drove over to the southeast area of Portland. Only God knew how to get to Zac's place that night, and He got us there miraculously.

When we arrived at the apartment, I went up to the door and knocked. It was about one in the morning. Zac's roommate, John, answered the door. John said Zac wasn't there so I decided to call him. When he answered his phone, I told him that I was at his place and that I needed to talk to him as soon as he could get there. Roger waited in his car.

About twenty minutes later Zac arrived. We walked toward each other and I'm sure he knew something was wrong.

"What happened, Dad?" he asked.

I hugged him and told him what no parent should ever have to utter, "Zac, your sister is dead. She was murdered earlier today." We cried together.

Standing outside the apartment Zac asked if his mom knew yet. She did not, I said. I told him that Detective Steight was waiting to get a call from us before he went to tell her. Zac expressed that he wanted to be the one to tell his mom. He was composed enough to get into his car and begin the hard journey to his mother's house. We followed part of the way to make sure Zac was okay.

Roger called the detective to let him know that Zac was on his way and to meet him outside his mom's house. Roger took me back to Hillsboro. It was about three in the morning when I arrived home. Julie was waiting for me. That was the first time that I began to plead with God to let me exchange places with Megan.

Where was Megan...heaven or...?

I did not know. I would gladly give up my life, my salvation, for my daughter.

I begged God again for answers, but He didn't respond.

CHAPTER 7
MOM AND JACK
COME TO OREGON

My mother and brother, Jack, come from Ohio each year in August to visit. However this particular year, 2006, they changed their trip from August to July 22. The day following Megan's murder. Only God could have known how much we would need them.

Jack was planning to stay for a week and Mom was staying for two weeks. I needed to call Mom and tell her the awful news. It was 3:30am pacific, 6:30am her time, when I called.

I don't remember much about our conversation. It was full of tears. I asked Mom not to come. I didn't want her to go through this horrible ordeal with Julie and I. I hung up the phone and saw Julie standing in front of me. She had an incredulous look on her face.

"Why don't you want your family to be with you, Tom?" she said. "This is what families are for, to be with you in times of sorrow and grief." Julie was right. I called Mom back and asked her to come. Mom had never intended to cancel the trip anyway. She knew where she needed to be. And wanted to be.

Julie and I then went to bed. I was dreading that moment when there would be complete darkness, silence and stillness. I prayed for peace and comfort. Amazingly, the next thing I remember, it was morning and I had slept soundly. God is good, all the time. God answers every prayer.

"If you believe, you will receive whatever you ask for in prayer." Matthew 21:22

But it was morning. Time to get up. Time to face the reality of the loss and sorrow. Time to get up. Time to get down on my knees and ask God for the strength to get through this day. It was Saturday, July 22, 2006 and we had to go pick up Mom and Jack at the airport.

Julie drove to the Portland airport. Waves of grief continued to flow over me. I had heard the term "waves of grief" before. Now I knew exactly what they were and how they felt. They truly were "waves." Like a huge wall of water completely submerging me in its power and overcoming me with sorrow and despair. Hopelessness in a sea of sorrow.

"Deep calls to deep, in the roar of your waterfalls; all your waves and breakers have swept over me." Psalm 42:7

There is a wonderful poem by Annie Johnson Flint that speaks of God's waves:

They are His billows, whether they go o'er us,
　　Hiding His face in smothering spray and foam;
　　Or smooth and sparkling, spread a path before us,
　　And to our haven bear us safely home.

They are His billows, whether for our succor
　　He walks across them, stilling all our fears;
　　Or to our cry there comes no aid nor answer,
　　And in the lonely silence none is near.

They are His billows, whether we are toiling

17

Through tempest-driven waves that never cease,
While deep to deep with clamor loud is calling;
Or at His work they hush themselves in peace.

They are His billows, whether He divides them,
Making us walk dryshod where seas had flowed;
Or lets tumultuous breakers surge about us,
Rushing unchecked across our only road.

They are His billows, and He brings us through them;
So He has promised, so His love will do.
Keeping and leading, guiding and upholding,
To His sure harbor, He will bring us through.

When we arrived at the airport, we went to the gate to meet them. As I saw Mom and Jack coming down the walkway I began to cry again. We met and embraced and cried together. Mom's grandchild had been murdered less than twenty-four hours ago. Jack's first niece was gone.

As we drove back to Hillsboro, there were many questions from Mom and Jack. What happened? How did it happen? Do the police have any leads? All the questions had the same answer.

We don't know.

CHAPTER 8
PASTOR PHIL

By the time we reached home, there were numerous messages on our phone. The word of Megan's death was spreading among family, friends and the public. The local news stations were running leads on television and radio, I was told. I chose not to watch or listen to any news coverage then, nor have I since. Local media tends to dwell on and feed off of personal tragedies. They sought me out but I refused to speak with them so as not to become part of their feeding frenzy.

I had made a few phone calls to close friends. One was to my pastor, Phil Comer. Pastor Phil is the senior pastor for Solid Rock, a Bible teaching church. Julie and I started attending Solid Rock in the fall of 2004 while they were meeting at a local middle school.

When we started going to Solid Rock, there were approximately two hundred fifty people attending. By 2006 there were close to seven hundred fifty people with two services on Sunday. Now there are over six thousand in attendance with four services on Sunday at a warehouse in Tigard, two services on Sunday evenings at a downtown Portland location and one service on Sunday in Hillsboro. The Holy Spirit is doing a miracle at Solid Rock.

Pastor Phil came to my house in the early afternoon of July 22. We talked and I told him what I knew. We went out on our deck that overlooks a verdant green space behind our house. As we were leaning on the deck railing Pastor Phil began to sing. It felt like I was being washed in a warm and comforting shower of love.

We talked and prayed together. Pastor Phil went back inside and I stayed on the deck. I fell to my knees in a desperate prayer to God asking why, again and again. I felt hopeless. I pleaded with God again to let me exchange places with Megan. I would gladly give up my salvation for Megan. I did not know where she was, heaven or hell. If she was in hell, I would go there in an instant, if God would let me.

As I was getting up from my knees, Julie brought me the phone. She said it was the Medical Examiner from Clackamas County. Detective Streight told me to be expecting a call from him within twenty-four hours. He would be calling to let me know the cause of death. He was now on the phone and had some information for me.

I was dreading this conversation but I knew I had to speak with him. The Medical Examiner told me how my daughter had died..."Megan was the victim of homicide and the cause of death was strangulation and multiple stab wounds."

His words rang in my ear like thunder. How can a parent withstand an assault of words like this? Like an echo, I kept hearing them over and over again.

My daughter, Megan, was the victim of a homicide. She had been strangled and stabbed to death. I did not know how long it had taken her to die and did not know the extent of her struggle until the closing arguments of the trial nearly two and a half years later. On July 22, 2006, I had no desire to know any of the specifics of her murder. God was protecting me.

I hung up the phone and wept. Julie came out to comfort me. I told her what happened.

Throughout the day friends stopped by the house to bring food and offer prayers of support. They were at a loss for words. There are no words in a time like that. But it didn't matter. Just the fact that people came by or called, brought comfort. It doesn't require words, just loving care.

About a year later at church, a friend approached me. He had tears in his eyes. He confessed, "Tom, I have been purposely avoiding you because I just didn't know what to say." He just wanted to say he was sorry. I hugged him and we cried. I told him that was all he needed to say.

We continued to have visitors throughout the day. Eventually, though, everyone left. Only Julie, Mom, Jack and I remained. Once again, I was dreading the night. The stillness. The darkness. The loneliness. The loss and sorrow. But God was there and I had a restful sleep.

During the days, weeks and months following, I would listen to Christian music on the radio in my car going to and from work. One song really became special to me. It touched my heart. I would break down every time it was played. I became very good at driving with an eyeful of tears. The song is called "You Never Let Go" and some of the words are:

Even though I walk through the valley of the shadow of death,
Your perfect love is casting out fear,
And even though when I'm caught in the middle of the storms
    of this life,
I won't turn back, I know you are near....

Oh no, You never let go, through the calm and through the
    storm,
Oh no, You never let go, in every high and every low,
Oh no, You never let go,
Lord, You never let go of me.[1]

---

1   See Appendix A

Chapter 9
The Birth of Drug Court

My heart for drug addicts was born out of Megan's use, abuse and addiction to numerous illegal drugs and alcohol. Megan began drinking alcohol in her early teens. Her drug use shortly followed. Marijuana and methamphetamine soon became her drugs of choice. Adding to Megan's problems was the fact that her mom and I divorced in 2000. Megan was angry with both of us and with her will of iron, there was little opportunity to change her direction.

When Megan was seventeen, I tried to get her into an intense inpatient program; the kind of program where the child is physically taken and forced to participate in confined residential treatment. It truly is a lock-down environment. This may seem harsh or unusual, but many children have been saved and rescued by this type of program. However, my plan for an intervention was unsuccsessful.

Megan would soon turn eighteen and no longer be eligible for this type of program that allowed children to be taken against their will. And we knew she wouldn't enter treatment on her own.

During this time, Julie and I were praying that God would take Megan to a place where she had no other direction to go, no other place to turn but to God. We also prayed for God to put people in her life that would show her how much He loved her and that His love was unconditional. We had been praying these prayers for her since 2000, when I first met Julie.

In the latter part of 2003, I was asked by the presiding judge of Washington County to head up a team of individuals to consider establishing a drug court for our county. We were looking for a better way to deal with the huge drug problem in our county.

We applied for and received federal funding to participate in training to establish it. The head of our local Community Corrections Department, John Hartner, and I flew to Jacksonville, Florida for our first training session in January of 2004. It was a three-day program and we absorbed as much information as we could about drug courts.

The first drug court in the United States was started in Miami, Florida. It began operating in 1989. The main purpose of drug court is to improve the outcomes of the criminal justice system as it encounters drug addicts and the crimes they commit. We know that locking a drug addict up in jail or prison is only a temporary solution. Eventually that person is going to get out and if nothing has changed in his/her heart, then the addiction and related criminal activity repeats itself time and time again.

Drug court combines treatment, counseling and accountability with the criminal justice system in an effort to change a person's life.[2] There are more than twenty-five hundred drug treatment courts operating in our country. Each one is different depending on the professionals that are involved. Statistics over the years have proven that drug courts reduce the rate of recidivism for offenders.

Drug courts across the country are helping substance abusing defendants stop using drugs and stop committing crimes. Through

---

2   See Ten Key Components of Drug Courts, Appendix B

a combination of judicial supervision, intense probation, treatment and counseling, mandatory drug testing, escalating sanctions and incentives and dedicated staffing teams, a huge impact on drug related recidivism has occurred.

The objective of drug court is clear: addicted offenders are connected to high intensity treatment; their progress is monitored by a drug court staffing team of attorneys, probation officers, treatment specialists, mentors and a judge. The participants engage in direct interaction with the judge who responds to progress and setbacks with a wide range of rewards and interventions. The successful participants have their charges dismissed, while those who fail receive agreed upon jail or prison sentences.[3]

We had two more training sessions in 2004 with our drug court planning team. We had no idea how our drug court was going to be funded. We applied for federal funding for $250,000 to cover the first year costs of the program for fifty participants. However we soon learned that our application for funding was denied. Once again, my plan had failed, but my prayer to trust in the Lord was soon to be answered.

"Commit to the Lord whatever you do, and your plans will succeed." Proverbs 16:3

In early 2005, we learned that the county was willing to provide some seed money for a drug court pilot program. The funding provided for only twenty participants. Jeff Peters, with the county Department of Human Services, was instrumental in securing the seed money. We were off and running. Our first official day operating as the Washington County Adult Treatment Drug Court was March 7, 2005. It was a Monday. Our drug court meets every Monday.

The mission statement for our drug court is: TO CHANGE PEOPLE'S LIVES, TO BREAK THE CYCLE OF ADDICTION, TO REUNITE THEM WITH THEIR FAMILIES AND TO PROMOTE COMMUNITY SAFETY. We, on the drug court

---

3   Drug Court Review, Volume VI, Issue 2, page 68

team, have been so blessed to see this mission accomplished with so many of our graduates.

Drug court represented and signified the hope I had for Megan's recovery.

CHAPTER 10
WASHINGTON COUNTY
DRUG COURT

Eligibility for drug court has several criteria. A participant must have an addiction to a drug and criminal charges must be pending against that person. The criminal charge(s) has to be a property crime such as identity theft, car theft or forgery to name just a few. We do not allow violent offenders into our program. The charges can be a misdemeanor (maximum sentence is less than a year in jail) or a felony (more than a year) or a combination of both. One of our participants had over thirty counts pending against her with five years in prison if she did not successfully complete drug court.

To begin drug court, the person must plead guilty to some, or all, of the charges. In some cases, all the charges will be dismissed if the participant successfully completes drug court. In other cases some of the charges may remain as a permanent record. It all depends on the prior criminal history and plea bargain that the defense attorney and district attorney enter into.

The minimum stay in our drug court is fifteen months. There is no maximum time within which to complete the program. Some participants have taken almost three years to graduate.

The program consists of five phases. We have ingeniously named them Phase 1, Phase 2, Phase 3, Phase 4 and Phase 5! We keep the participants busy by filling each day with programs involving treatment, counseling and job search. We also require them to attend Narcotics Anonymous (NA) and/or Alcoholic Anonymous (AA) meetings. They need to attend at least three of these meetings per week. One of these meetings can be a church service. Many of our participants are followers of Jesus. Some have gone astray. Others are new believers who have accepted Jesus as their Lord and Savior while in drug court. At one of our graduations, we had a local pastor come to talk about the graduate. The graduate was attending his church. Scripture references and the name of Jesus came with the pastor's remarks. A woman from my church was in the courtroom observing drug court that day. After the graduation she came up to me and said, "Judge, I don't know why anyone is not picketing outside your courtroom door!" I responded that God was protecting us during that season of time.

And He still is!

I have had the opportunity and blessing to pray with many of the drug court participants in my chambers. I feel so honored that God would trust me with this privilege.

A beginning participant in Phase 1 is required to appear in court every Monday afternoon. As they transition through the program to Phases 4 and 5, they are only required to appear once a month. We gradually let go of the apron string.

In the beginning most participant's brains are still foggy from months and years of drug abuse. Many began using drugs and alcohol when they were in their early teens; some even before their teenage years. The ages of participants in our drug court have ranged from twenty-one to sixty-two.

The participants are also required to submit to random body substance testing. Usually testing comes by way of a urinalysis (UA). UA techs are required to watch the liquid come out of the hole, as crude as that may sound. You can imagine how uncomfortable this would be for all involved. One time the test results came back as non-human. It was tea. We later discovered that the UA tech did not watch the procedure properly!

Drug addicts are very resourceful in the ways they try to beat a UA test. Sometimes they will have friends pee in a bottle for them. They put the bottle under their arm pit to keep it warm and then pour the liquid into the receptacle. Once again, this is why the test needs to be observed!

Participants are required to live in clean and sober housing. One option in our county is a nationally recognized drug-free housing program known as Oxford Houses. These houses are independently governed by their own residents. They are required to give random drug testing on themselves without supervision. A dirty UA requires immediate removal from the home. The UA tests are only as reliable as the residents are honest.

There are other local clean and sober housing options, such as Homeward Bound and Bridges to Change. There are also faith-based homes like House of Hope and Fairhaven. The faith-based homes include daily Bible studies for their residents.

Participants are also required to obtain employment. This helps them gain back some self esteem and allows for payment of restitution to victims of their crimes. Over $95,000 has been returned to victims (as of this writing) since drug court started in 2005.

In addition to restitution, the public is the beneficiary of saving millions of dollars for the cost of prison beds. As I said earlier, many participants have prison time hanging over their heads if they do not successfully complete drug court. These are crimes they would have been sentenced and imprisoned on, but for the drug court opportunity. It costs about $30,000 per year to house an inmate in our state prison system. Our drug court has diverted over one hundred fifty years of prison time over the life of the program so far. That equates to $4,500,000!

Our drug court is unique. As I mentioned earlier, each drug court is different. Some work only with first-time offenders. We believe that our county probation department can work with first-time offenders effectively. Therefore, we have consciously chosen to work with high risk, high need defendants who have significant criminal histories and significant drug addictions. The drugs of choice for participants in our program are generally marijuana, methamphetamine, cocaine and heroin.

We have a group of professionals that meet every Monday for two hours to discuss each participant in the program. The staffing team consists of treatment counselors, probation officers, mentors who are former addicts, a defense attorney, a deputy district attorney, a childrens' services case worker, a deputy sheriff and myself. For the first time in our client's lives, they have a group of caring and invested professionals gathered around a table discussing how they can help the clients succeed.

During the staffing session, we review how each participant has performed the week prior. We consider sanctions for negative behavior and rewards for positive behavior. We come to a general consensus as to how each client should be dealt with during the drug court session.

One of the most effective tools found in drug court is the use of progressive sanctioning. The first principle of sanctioning is that it has to be swift and certain. For example if you wait two weeks to discipline your child for disobeying, it is seldom if ever effective. They have forgotten the behavior by then! The discipline needs to happen as close as possible in time to the conduct involved.

In drug court the sanctioning also has to be progressive. We don't throw someone in jail for missing an appointment with a counselor. Rather, a written assignment directly related to the undesired conduct would be the first sanction. For a second offense, then maybe a half day of community service would be warranted and so on.

For dirty UAs, the first sanction is always a loss of the participant's clean days. The total amount of clean days for drug court participants is a source of pride and confirmation that they are headed in the right direction. A loss of clean days always stings. A second dirty UA, may require the participant to attend thirty AA or NA meetings in thirty days which is a significant increase in the usual three meetings per week. The next sanction might involve daily UA testing for a few weeks or a short stint in our local jail. Lastly, intensive inpatient treatment may be necessary. If this fails, then removal from drug court may occur. We try to make it very difficult for someone to fail and be taken out of drug court. Drug court is a court of second, third and fourth chances.

We want them to succeed.

During the actual court session, each participant comes before me to discuss his or her prior week. I call them by their first name which would never happen in regular court. After a discussion about how they are doing, they walk back to the seating area while everyone in the courtroom applauds them for the effort they have made.

Drug court is an upside down world. Where would you see a prosecutor clapping her hands in support of a criminal defendant? Where would you see a deputy sheriff doing the same, or a probation officer, or a judge? Only in drug court! It is an amazing experience. Go observe a drug court in action. More than likely, there is one close to you. More on drug court later.

Needless to say, Megan was my inspiration for establishing drug court and for wanting to be part of God's program for second and third and fourth chances in this life.

I love drug court...can you tell?

Megan loved to play in the mud.

And play with the water hose.

Megan loved animals, especially her kitty.

She was a special dresser!

Megan and Zac (in camo)...can you see him?

The snowman looks a little forlorn.

On her Dad's shoulders...one of her favorite places as a child.

Megan and Shammy, our chocolate lab.

Smiles galore!

Her first communion.

A little sassy.

Good memories.

A beautiful young woman.

Her Shar-Pei.

Winsome.

Megan and Zac...good buddies.

May 31, 1985, to July 21, 2006

Chapter 11
The Rescuer

When Megan was in 5th grade, she made some business cards to pass out to classmates, friends and even strangers. I would call Megan a "rescuer." She was one of those special people who was drawn to the down and out. She would always come to the aid of someone who was being victimized by bullies. She had an immeasurable empathy for fellow classmates who were different, who came from broken homes. She was drawn to them.

The business cards had Megan's name, address and phone number on them with an invitation stating, "...if you need a good friend, call Megan." She would readily befriend the outcasts of our community, the lost, the hurting and the afflicted. Megan would empathize with them and encourage them. She had a compassionate heart, a heart like Jesus, at the young age of ten.

Appearing in front of me every day are the lost, the afflicted, the hurting and the outcast of our community. I have a scripture on my bench in my courtroom in a small, black frame that proclaims..."For the Son of Man came to seek and to save what was lost." Luke 19:10. This scripture serves to remind me of the heart Jesus has for the lost (that same heart that Megan had) and prompts me to pray for them.

The problem with Megan being a rescuer became more apparent as she grew older. She immersed herself into the lives of the people she was drawn to. Unfortunately, some of those people were drug addicts.

Soon Megan was using drugs. She could not maintain the boundary between helping another human being and exposing herself to extreme danger. She began using drugs with the same people she cared so much for and soon her drug use became a full-blown addiction. She became addicted to methamphetamine.

Cocaine has been around for hundreds of years. Meth is relatively new in that it has been used in the drug world for only several decades. Ingesting cocaine will give the user a high for about forty-five minutes to an hour. Ingesting meth will create a high many times greater, lasting up to ten to twelve hours. It is relatively cheap on the street. A dose can be purchased for less than $10. And you can buy it any place including bus stops, bars, street corners, church parking lots, courthouse grounds and school yards.

Methamphetamine is made from poisons and common household ingredients. People make it in their basements, bedrooms, kitchens and garages. There are also mobile meth labs. Some of these are found in vans and trunks of cars.

Here are some of the ingredients often found in meth. Imagine putting any of these up your nose, in your mouth or in your blood veins:

Alcohol	Red Phosphorous
Gasoline additives/Rubbing alcohol	Brake cleaner
Ether (starting fluid)	Red Devil lye
Benzene	Drain cleaner
Paint thinner	Muraitic acid
Freon	Battery acid

Acetone

Chloroform

Camp stove fuel

White gasoline

Cold tablets

Diet aids

Iodine crystals

Lithium from batteries

Anhydrous ammonia

Rock or Epsom salt

Sodium metal

Iodine

Ephedrine

When meth is being produced ("cooked" in drug terms), certain lab equipment is necessary and could include a combination of the following: plastic tubing, Mason jars with tubes attached, coffee filters, two liter plastic pop bottles, blenders, wooden matches, propane cylinders and hot plates.[4]

Recently new legislation across the country has managed to make it more difficult for meth cooks to get some of the chemicals from off the shelf in drug and grocery stores. For example, ephedrine, often found in cold medicine is no longer available on the shelf in Oregon. But for the most part, the ingredients are still obtainable. It is not hard to imagine the damage that can be done to a person's brain by any combination of the above ingredients. Some people have used meth for fifteen years or more. Some use it daily. Megan used it for more than five years.

---

4   METH Awareness and Prevention Project of South Dakota

CHAPTER 12
THE FUNERAL

Megan's funeral was scheduled for July 26, 2006, at the same Catholic church where she was baptized, christened and took her first communion. My sister, Mary, had flown into Portland two days before. My entire immediate family was here to support Julie and myself.

Julie and I had just moved into our new home in Hillsboro, Oregon on July 7, exactly two weeks before Megan's murder. Previously we lived outside of town on a ridge top in a fairly secluded area. We had lived there since getting married in 2001, and according to all public records, that location was still our residence.

I learned several days after the funeral that the local television stations had gone to our previous residence to camp out the morning of the funeral to, I assume, try to catch us for an interview or video us on our way to the funeral. The Washington County Presiding Judge's daughter was murdered. They wanted to interview me. I was so thankful that they did not know where our new home was located.

We arrived at the church an hour or so before the funeral ceremony was to begin. I saw Megan's mom. We hugged and cried. I was told that there were close to five hundred people at Megan's funeral. The Chief Justice of the Oregon Supreme Court attended along with most of my colleagues on the bench from Washington County. The Washington County Sheriff and the Washington County District Attorney were also in attendance.

Megan was especially close to Judge Mark Gardner. Mark and I were friends before I became a judge. Megan and Mark used to play gin rummy together. When I saw Mark at the funeral we hugged each other tightly and cried. I had never seen Mark cry before.

I had tremendous support from my colleagues during this trying time. During one of our monthly meetings in the fall of 2006, the judges presented me with a plaque in honor of Megan. They gave a substantial sum of money to drug court in her name. I will forever be grateful for their kindness.

Several people spoke at the funeral. Zac was the most compelling. He spoke about the loss of his sister, the loss of his friend. He had so much composure as a young man, a son and a brother. I did not speak. I could not speak. I could not believe it was happening. It did not seem real. I could only ask...why God? I continued begging God to let me trade places with Megan.

Please, God.

Pastor Phil was permitted by the Catholic priest to speak on behalf of my family. He was not permitted to give a gospel message, but was allowed to sing a worship song, a beautiful rendition of Amazing Grace. He was also allowed to read a statement from Julie and I. This was the statement that we prepared for the funeral:

Thank you all for being here today. We greatly appreciate the phone calls, flowers, cards and food that have been delivered to our home to minister to us in this time.

No words can describe the unbearable pain in this tragic loss of Megan that brings us together today. We cannot possibly wrap our minds around what has happened. My sorrow runs deeper than I can comprehend...I miss her intensely. She had such a compassionate heart, a heart like Jesus. Megan would, without hesitation, befriend the outcast of our community, the lost, the hurting, the afflicted. Megan would suffer with them and encourage them. When she was in the 5th grade, she had some business cards made. The cards had her name and her phone number on them, with an invitation stating '...if you need a good friend, call Megan.'

There is a deep hole in our hearts today that will, some day, begin to fill with the grace, mercy and the peace of God. Thank you for your powerful prayers that have sustained us during this time.

We find comfort in God and His promises in the book of Psalms:

I cry out to God and the Lord hears me He delivers me from all my troubles
The Lord is close to the brokenhearted and saves those who are crushed in spirit.

Oh, God, Remember your word to your servant, for you have given me hope.
My comfort in my suffering is this: Your promise preserves my life.

Trust in Him at all times, O people pour out your hearts to Him, for

God is our refuge and our strength, a very present
help in trouble.

After the service today, we invite you to join us at
our home for food and fellowship.

We were not permitted to have any references to the Psalms in
our message. Pastor Phil read the message omitting the Psalms.

There were also some security issues at the funeral. The
Washington County Sheriff's Office was taking every precaution
to make sure no one interrupted it. There was an obvious police
presence in uniform in the parking lot and around the outside of the
church and a not so obvious group of undercover officers stationed
inside and out because the killer was still at large.

Julie and I were so blessed by the huge attendance at Megan's
funeral. Those who came to support us included our family
members and people from the courthouse, the district attorney's
office, the probation office, the sheriff's office, members of other
law enforcement communities, Julie's fellow employees from the Art
Institute of Portland, our family at Solid Rock Church, neighbors
and my drug court staffing team and participants.

When the funeral was over, we went home to a house full of
friends and family. Many women from Solid Rock had stayed back at
our home to prepare food for the gathering after the funeral. The rest
of the day and evening was filled with sweet fellowship and prayer.

*Thank you, Father, for the fellowship of believers that is only possible
through the power of your Holy Spirit.*

One scripture that would profoundly change my heart and
encourage me as time went by was 2 Corinthians 1:3-7:

Praise be to the God and Father of our Lord Jesus
Christ, the Father of compassion and the God of
all comfort, who comforts us in all our troubles, so

that we can comfort those in any trouble with the comfort we ourselves have received from God. For just as the sufferings of Christ flow over into our lives, so also through Christ our comfort overflows. If we are distressed, it is for your comfort and salvation; if we are comforted, it is for your comfort, which produces in you patient endurance of the same sufferings we suffer. And our hope for you is firm, because we know that just as you share in our sufferings, so also you share in our comfort.

I became intensely aware of one commonality between God and me...we both had children that were murdered. Eventually I would have many opportunities to comfort others with the same comfort that I received from God.

There was still no word from the Clackamas County District Attorney's office on the status of the murder investigation. There would be no contact from them for several months. It felt like an eternity.

CHAPTER 13
THE CHANGE

I was raised a Methodist and converted to a Catholic in 1983 when Zac was born. I had heard the name of Jesus many times but didn't have a personal relationship with Him until I was fifty-three years old.

I attended the University of Kentucky on a football scholarship. During my time at UK, I was using drugs and alcohol to the point where my college career was in jeopardy. I got to know the Dean of Men quite well! I dropped out of college after my third year and joined the Peace Corps in 1968.

The Peace Corps provided an opportunity for me to take a break and have a small impact on a tribal community in northern India. The tribe was known as the Santalis. I was stationed with a Jesuit Catholic missionary priest. I spent almost two years in India and returned to the United States with a more mature attitude. I went back to UK and graduated with a BA degree in English literature.

My goal was to become an English literature professor, but I did poorly on the Graduate Records Examination. Ironically, my high school English teacher once predicted that I would become a lawyer some day, so I took the law school examination and did well. I entered law school in the fall of 1972 and graduated three years later, in the top ten percent...of the lower half of my class. Law school was not easy for me.

I practiced law in a small Ohio town for seven years. I was married while in law school, but divorced a few short years after graduation. I remarried and my second wife, Teresa, and I moved to Oregon in 1982. I had stopped using drugs by this point in my life.

As I mentioned earlier, Zac was born in 1983 and Megan in 1985. I had a financially successful law practice and was appointed to a judgeship in 1997. I knew *of* Jesus through my Methodist upbringing and Catholic conversion, but I didn't *know* Jesus as evidenced by my worldly desires and harshness with Teresa and my children. I was unforgiving, self-centered, vengeful and aggressive in my style of practice. I still look back at my life prior to Jesus and feel regret, even though I know Jesus has forgiven me for my past, present and future sins.

Teresa and I were separated in 1999 and divorced in 2000. Another failed marriage, except this time there were two children who had to suffer the consequences of this failure. A feeling of hopelessness began to permeate my life.

In August of 2000, I met a woman who would eventually be part of a huge change in my life. Her name was Julie. She was different from any other woman I knew. We began dating casually, but it was different this time. Unlike my previous relationships with women, there was no sleeping together. She told me she was a believer and a follower of Jesus Christ. A Christian.

Darn, no sex with this one unless or until I married her!

Previously, I thought I was a Christian, but soon discovered there was an eternal difference between claiming to be a "Christian" and actually having a personal relationship with Jesus, the living God.

I found myself attending church with Julie on a regular basis. The church was a Calvary Chapel, a Jesus-centered church. My heart started to change as I heard the gospel message from our pastor every Sunday. I later looked back and discovered that as I was falling in love with Julie, I was also falling in love with Jesus.

At the end of October of 2000, I was asked by a friend if I wanted to attend a men's retreat at Camp Bradley in Bandon, Oregon. Sounded like fun. A group of guys meeting on the beautiful southern Oregon coast. Eating together, worshipping together and hearing some good preaching.

I was getting weird.

One of the pastors at the retreat was Jason Mandaro. Jason was a young surfer from California. He had started a small Calvary Chapel that had mid-week services in the Portland area. Jason was teaching through the Book of Acts. He also led worship with a guitar and wore flip flops and jeans!

The retreat began on November 3, 2000. My friend and I arrived late in the afternoon. It was Friday. There were probably thirty to thirty-five men from a couple of different churches. We ate supper together and then regrouped in the chapel for evening services.

That evening my life changed forever. I heard the message of the good news in a way that I had never heard before. I confessed my sins, I accepted Jesus as my Lord and Savior and truly knew that He had given up his life for me. All the sins that I had previously committed and all my future sins were forgiven by His death on the cross. I believed that He had risen from the grave on the third day and He now sits at the right hand of God interceding for all of us.

The good news to me was "...if you confess with your mouth, Jesus is Lord, and believe in your heart that God raised Him from the dead, you will be saved." Romans 10:9. I was fifty-three years old and had just been born again! But someone was not very pleased with my decision to have a personal relationship with Jesus. His name was Satan and his attacks began immediately in earnest. He had me for fifty-three years and was not going to go away quietly.

The evening of November 3rd was difficult. Pastor Jason and the other men gathered around me and prayed. As Satan's attacks were driven away by the prayers of the men at the retreat, I was able to settle into a peace that I had never known. I was beginning to understand what Paul said in Philippians 4:7. "And the peace of God, which transcends all understanding, will guard your hearts and your minds in Christ Jesus."

I called Julie from the coast and told her what had happened. There were tears of joy!

Ten days later as I was going into the courthouse for the beginning of a work day I was filled with the Holy Spirit. It was like I was being filled from the inside out. I was literally overflowing with the Spirit just as the disciples were at Pentecost ten days after Christ's ascension as recorded in Acts, Chapter 2! That morning I will never forget.

I was assigned to the arraignment court. There were more than fifty defendants who had to appear in front of me that morning to hear charges that were brought against them. My job was to explain their rights to them and schedule the next date for them to appear in court. As each defendant's case was called I could see the face of Jesus in each of them. God had given me new eyes to see with.

My courtship with Julie became serious at that point. On December 31, 2000 I asked her to marry me. We were married on August 31, 2001.

Zac and Megan attended the wedding. I know it was hard on them to see their dad get married after being divorced from their mom. Divorce has consequences that no divorced couple ever intend. Megan became more distant as time went by. I tried to share the joy of Christ with her, but she was not ready. Her drug abuse continued. I was only able to stay in touch with her by phone and only if she wanted to answer a call from me.

But I was a changed man. I wanted to love my children like I never had before. Even if they didn't want to listen, I wanted to be the hands and feet of Jesus to them, demonstrate Christ's love to them and pray for them.

CHAPTER 14
HOPE

As I mentioned earlier, the Washington County Adult Drug Court began officially on March 7, 2005. In February of that year I had an opportunity to attend a one-day seminar at Portland State University. The seminar focused on methamphetamine; its use, abuse, addiction and pharmacology. It was attended by treatment counselors, alcohol and addiction specialists, probation officers and some police. I spoke with several of the participants and learned about their backgrounds and areas of expertise. They were also interested in hearing about our new drug court in Washington County.

I was asked by the facilitator to speak briefly at the beginning of the afternoon session on the format of our drug court. I telephoned Julie during the lunch hour and we prayed about what I should say.

There were more than one hundred people at the seminar. When it came time to speak, I talked about our format. I spoke about our drug court being a court of second and third and fourth chances, just like our Father in heaven is the God of second and third and fourth chances. You could hear a pin drop when I finished. For the rest of the afternoon, not a person spoke to me. As I was leaving, a fellow from Eugene approached and thanked me for acknowledging God in my brief presentation. To most of the people in attendance at that seminar the words I spoke must have seemed like gibberish. It reminded me of 1 Corinthians 1:18. "For the message of the cross is foolishness to those who are perishing, but to us who are being saved it is the power of God."

Our first participant in drug court was Erica. She had been referred to our drug court by a judge from another county. She was a heroin addict and had several property crimes pending against her.

Erica was pregnant with her third child at the time. Our Children Services Department had been involved in the birth of her first two children. Erica did not have custody of them because of her drug addiction and criminal history. Both children had been placed with a family relative.

Our drug court staffing and treatment team was able to get Erica involved in treatment and counseling about a month before our first court session. Erica was doing well and she wanted to keep this baby. She was scheduled to attend our first drug court session on March 7, 2005, but she didn't make it to court. She was in the hospital having her new baby boy. And he was drug free! This was her first child to be drug free at birth.

We were so proud of Erica and her determination to get clean and sober for her baby and for herself. She was in drug court for about two years. She even had another baby while in drug court. He was also drug free. I saw her recently at our annual drug court picnic and she looked great. Her two young boys also came. They were healthy and rambunctious. She was still clean and sober!

Erica was a perfect example of our drug court mission; her life had been changed, she broke the cycle of addiction, she was reunited with her family and she had not committed any new crimes. The community was safe and so was Erica and her children.

Within several months we had twenty participants in the pilot program. I was excited about the prospects of being part of a program that had such a huge impact on the lives of individuals and families. In the meantime I knew Megan was struggling tremendously with her addiction. There was nothing I could do except pray that God would protect her and take her to a place where she had nowhere to turn but to Him. Julie and I were relentless in our prayers for Megan.

At one point, I learned that Megan was interested in treatment for her addiction. Arrangements were made to enroll her in an intensive outpatient program nearby. It was a thirty-day program. I knew Megan needed more than that, but I would jump at any chance to see her get some treatment. She attended the program, had one relapse that I knew about, and eventually completed it. Shortly after completing the outpatient program Megan was using meth again.

Our prayers for Megan intensified.

I knew that God had given me a chance to be a parent again through drug court. I thank Him every day for this opportunity. Megan was not in my life at this point, but I knew that prayer moved the hand of God and I was praying incessantly for my daughter.

I knew there was hope.

Why are you so downcast, O my soul?
Why so disturbed within me?
Put your HOPE in God,
for I will yet praise Him,
my Savior and my God. Psalm 42:5.

There was only one person to put my hope in, and that was Jesus.

My other prayer for Megan was that she would be arrested by the police. Megan was not accountable to anyone. Not to her mom, not to me. I was hoping that she would be brought into the criminal justice system so that she would have a probation officer, someone that she would be accountable to. For those parents who have children with drug problems, this is not an unusual prayer. For those parents who don't have this issue, consider yourselves blessed.

I had several conversations with another drug court judge about Megan. If she was arrested in the metropolitan area, then maybe she could get into his drug court. We both knew drug court worked. Julie and I were praying for divine police intervention. I continued to call Megan every week. Sometimes she would answer her phone and speak to me, but most of the time she wouldn't. I persisted with my phone calls to her, to pursue her, just as God pursued me.

CHAPTER 15
DRUG COURT'S FIRST
GRADUATE

Our first drug court graduate was Jeri. She had been employed in the health care profession for several years and did not have a criminal history until she began using drugs in her mid-thirties. She was a nurse and was the owner of three adult care foster homes.

Eventually Jeri was using methamphetamine on a daily basis. She was injecting it into her arms. She lost her job because of her addiction. She started to hang out with criminals and soon was committing property crimes to help pay for her drugs. The crimes became more frequent.

Jeri would get arrested, released from jail because of overcrowding, and then arrested again for committing new crimes while she was out on release. This cycle is a typical scenario for a drug addict. She began to know the police on a first name basis. Her crimes included forgery, identity theft, theft and possession of forged instruments.

During her crime spree years, Jeri was incarcerated for at least six years on identity theft and drug related charges. She was a significant crime figure in Washington County.

Her face had the typical open sores found on meth users. Each time she was arrested, there was a booking photo taken of her. She was extremely thin. Meth robs one's appetite. Her last arrest before drug court involved over thirty separate crimes. She was looking at ten years in prison if she was convicted on all counts. She heard about drug court while she was in custody in the Washington County jail. Jeri was interested. Our drug court coordinator met with her in jail. Jeri decided to try to get into drug court. A deal was made with the district attorney's office and she was allowed to enter drug court. But if she failed, then she would be sentenced by me to five years in prison.

Jeri was ready to change. She had seen her life spiral downward in a few short years. She had lost everything. Her only hope was drug court. When new people come into drug court I ask them if they are ready to become responsible, accountable and honest. I call it the RAH factor. We can tell quite early in the program if someone truly wants to change. It's the RAH factor that becomes apparent with each participant. Jeri was ready for RAH.

Jeri embraced her recovery from the beginning. She had a job within thirty days from entering drug court. She began working at a local bakery in Beaverton. She was able to pay all of her financial obligations by the time she graduated. All of her UAs were negative. Jeri sailed through drug court and graduated one year after entering our program.

Our first drug court graduate!

Beaverton Bakery started a program that hires persons who are in recovery from alcohol and drug addiction. It also actively supports the reentry process of individuals from prison to our community

Jeri is now the general manager of Beaverton Bakery. She even hires some of our drug court participants.

We have been richly blessed by this very generous bakery. Beaverton Bakery has graciously supplied all of our graduation cakes since the very beginning; more than one hundred twelve cakes.

CHAPTER 16
THE FIRST ATTEMPT

M egan struggled in high school. She was having problems with some of her classmates and eventually withdrew from school. She enrolled in community college where she was able to obtain her high school degree and earn some college credits.

She did not attend the community college very long. She began skipping classes and getting incompletes in her course work. She was getting more and more involved in the drug culture. This was a dangerous place to be. The people she was hanging out with were addicts and dealers. Soon she became involved in selling drugs and the darkness of that world began to envelop her. She was becoming part of the lost. It was more difficult for me to have any contact with her.

When Megan started dating a Laotian gang member, her life spiraled out of control. Some of those gang members had appeared in front of me at court, though I did not know that they were connected at the time. The Laotian gangs are known for their violence.

On July 11, 2004, I arrived home in the early evening from spending some time with Zac. Julie mentioned that Detective

Dennis Marley from the Beaverton Police Department had called for me. Julie told me that it was important that I call him as soon as possible.

Detective Marley told me that someone had tried to kill Megan earlier that day. He was trying to locate Megan because she fled from her apartment and was not answering her cell phone. He wanted to give me an update. The television news was all over the story because Megan's father was the Presiding Judge. Marley wanted to make sure I heard about the details from him first.

The police eventually learned that a murder contract had been put out on Megan and her Laotian boyfriend by a rival Hispanic gang. A Hispanic male and female had gone to Megan's apartment to kill her. Megan had left just minutes before their arrival. Megan's roommate reported that she was walking up the stairway to their apartment when she saw the Hispanic couple standing at her front door.

The woman asked if Megan was home. The roommate responded "No" but she might be able to catch Megan in the parking lot because Megan had just left. The woman asked what color Megan's car was. "Blue" was her response.

The roommate told the investigators that she then went into the apartment and began to make lunch. She used her cell phone to text Megan about the couple. Almost immediately she received a call from Megan wanting to know who was asking for her. The roommate described the couple. Megan didn't recognize either one.

About five minutes later, she heard someone knocking on the front door. As she went to the door, it was forced open rapidly and the man rushed into the apartment.

Megan's dog, a Shar-Pei, was in the apartment and it began to bark and growl at the intruder. He pulled a small handgun out of his pocket and immediately shot at the dog. The shooter missed.

At that point the roommate saw a chance to escape and ran out the front door. Behind her, the roommate heard three or four shots being fired. As she was running down the stairs she called 9-1-1. Dozens of Beaverton police officers responded to the scene.

After the 9-1-1 call, the roommate realized she was in extreme pain. Her right shoulder was injured. She was taken to the hospital where it was determined that she had a gunpowder burn on her shoulder. She also had a temporary loss of hearing due to her proximity to the gun when it was fired. Later, it was determined by an expert that the gun had to be less than twenty-four inches from the roommate at the time it was fired.

Detective Marley told me that the Beaverton Police Department had more than thirty detectives and patrol officers working on the case. They knew that Megan was not harmed and they wanted to talk to her as soon as possible. I gave him her phone number, but it was the same number he already had for her. Megan was not answering her phone.

The criminal investigation had begun. There was an all-out effort to apprehend the people responsible for this crime. Detective Marley kept me informed on a daily basis.

Megan was found later that evening. The police made arrangements to meet with her and her Laotian boyfriend at a restaurant in Portland. After they met, Detective Marley called and told me that Megan was reluctant to talk. It appeared that the presence of her boyfriend at the restaurant was part of the reason for her reluctance.

Some time later I was told by a police officer friend, that if he ever committed a crime, the one person he would not want to investigate it was Detective Marley. He referred to him as a "pit bull."

I was very pleased to hear that description of Detective Marley!

The Beaverton Police Department did an awesome job of tracking down leads and interviewing potential witnesses. Detective Marley made every effort to keep me informed as to the status of the investigation. There was a lot of pressure put on some gang members in the community. Marley found out the name of a gang member who might have put the contract out on Megan. He had an informant who was willing to have a body wire put on him to get a confession from the suspect.

A meeting was set up between the informant and the suspect. The informant had the body wire on him and went to the meeting place, a bar in the Beaverton area. But there was one major problem. The battery on the body wire was dead! So Marley had to set up the meeting again.

A second meeting was arranged between the informant and the suspect. This time it worked. The suspect admitted that he paid $3500 to have someone kill Megan and her boyfriend. The police had sufficient statements from the suspect, Cesar Reyes, Jr. to take the case before a Washington County Grand Jury.

During the investigation and interrogation, Reyes refused to identify the shooter. He was rightfully afraid of retribution.

The district attorney in charge of this case was Roger Hanlon.

CHAPTER 17
TRIAL AND COMFORT

The grand jury system in the United States came from the common law of England over three hundred years ago. The modern day purpose of the grand jury is to review evidence presented by the district attorney and to determine whether there has been a crime committed and whether the person being investigated committed the crime.

The original purpose of the grand jury was to act as a buffer between the king (and his prosecutors) and the citizens of the local community.[5] Today it is used as an investigative tool which ultimately decides whether to issue an indictment. An indictment is the charging document that essentially starts the case in our criminal justice system.

In Washington County, the grand jury consists of five to seven jurors who are randomly selected from the general jury pool. Their term of service lasts for five weeks unless it is extended. The proceedings of the grand jury are secret. Those jurors on the grand

---

5   American Bar Association, http://www.abanet.org

jury are not allowed to talk about any case that comes before them. Over half of the states in our country employ the use of some form of the grand jury system.

Hanlon presented the case to the grand jury. The grand jury returned an indictment against Cesar Reyes, Jr. He was charged with Solicitation to Commit Murder, Attempted Aggravated Murder, Attempted Murder and Assault in the First Degree against Megan and her roommate.

He was arrested and bail was set at $500,000. Reyes could not post the necessary amount to get out of jail so he remained in custody.

An out-of-county judge was assigned to the case and trial was scheduled for the spring of 2005. The courtroom for the trial was on the same floor as my courtroom. Both Marley and Hanlon kept me up to date on the status of the case.

The trial began on April 19, 2005 and ended on April 22. Megan did not testify at trial but her roommate did. Megan was in hiding. I believed that she continued to fear for her life. The jury returned a verdict of guilty on the charges of Attempted Murder and Assault in the First Degree involving Megan's roommate. The jury came back with a not guilty verdict on the charges of Solicitation to Commit Murder and Attempted Aggravated Murder involving Megan. The defendant was sentenced to one hundred fifteen months in prison.

The shooter was never identified.

From this point on it became more difficult for me to have any contact with Megan. She would seldom answer her phone when I called. If she did answer, the conversation was short. Megan was becoming more and more isolated from family. Julie and I continued to pray for her. We prayed that she would be brought into the criminal justice system so she would be accountable to someone.

Some people may think that praying for your child to be arrested is wrong. I believe that those of us parents who have children lost in the dark and dangerous world of drugs, pray the same prayer. We desperately desire to have our children break the cycle of addiction, even if it is through the light of the criminal justice system. I meet parents of addicted children on a regular basis who pray this way.

There have been numerous occasions when I have had the opportunity to pray with parents whose children appeared in front of me for sentencing on drug and related charges. Often I see parents in the courtroom fearful for their children who are going to jail. I can sense the desperation that each parent feels. At the end of the court session I invite them back into my chambers to talk about what happened. I tell them about Megan and how they are so blessed that they still have a chance to be part of their child's recovery.

I encourage them to be hopeful.

Each time I cry as I tell the story of Megan and her addiction to methamphetamine and the ultimate price she paid. The parents sit weeping as I pray for them and their child in my chambers. God gives them hope through the story of Megan. God has given me hope too. I am able to comfort them with the same comfort that God gave me during the days, weeks, months and years since Megan was murdered.

> Praise be to the God and Father of our Lord Jesus Christ, the Father of compassion and the God of all comfort, who comforts us in all our troubles, so that we can comfort those in any trouble with the comfort we ourselves have received from God. 2 Corinthians 1:3-5

As I look back at these moments with the parents of drug-addicted children, I can see the hand of God in each instance. He is using this tragedy to give them hope. Each encounter reminds me again of the truth found in Romans 8:28:

"And we know that in all things God works for the good of those who love him, who have been called according to his purpose."

I count myself blessed that God has chosen to place me in a position in the workplace in which I have opportunities to pray with parents, victims of crimes and our drug court participants. I have a depth of understanding now, more than ever before, on trials and how God uses them in our lives; he turns tragedies into triumphs!

"Therefore, since we have been justified through faith, we have peace with God through our Lord Jesus Christ, through whom we have gained access by faith into this grace in which we now stand. And we rejoice in the HOPE of the glory of God. Not only so, but we also rejoice in our SUFFERINGS, because we know that suffering produces PERSEVERANCE, perseverance, CHARACTER; and character, HOPE. And hope does not disappoint us, because God has poured out his love into our hearts by the Holy Spirit, whom he has given us. (Emphasis added) Romans 5:1-5

CHAPTER 18
RADD'S STORY

Radd was another drug court graduate. He came into drug court with a two-year prison sentence hanging over his head. He was a longtime meth addict. He was thirty-two years old and had been using meth for more than eighteen years.

When Radd was about eight years old he witnessed his father shoot and kill his stepmother in a bedroom. Then his father put the handgun in his mouth and committed suicide in front of Radd and his older brother. His stepmother actually lived for about forty-five minutes after she was shot in the throat. Radd remembered blood splattered all over the bedroom. This murder-suicide took place in California. Radd was taken into custody by childrens' services. He was placed with his biological mother in a small town in southern Oregon. His mother was an alcoholic.

Soon Radd began to use and abuse alcohol at the age of nine. The alcohol was easily accessible to Radd and his friends. By the time Radd reached eleven years old, he was a full blown alcoholic.

At twelve, Radd was smoking marijuana on a daily basis and eventually graduated to meth. He was in and out of juvenile detention centers during this time. He never finished high school.

When he turned eighteen years old, he inherited $500,000 from his father's estate. Within one year, Radd had blown it all on drugs and gambling. He married during this time. After that money was gone, his wife inherited a substantial sum of money from her family. This money was gone within six months.

Radd was in and out of prison four times between the ages of eighteen and thirty. When he was out of prison, he was doing meth. When he was in prison, he wasn't. He didn't learn anything about recovery while he served time in the state prison system. By the time Radd was thirty and while he was in custody in the Washington County jail waiting to resolve new criminal charges his heart started to change. That is when he heard about drug court. He wanted in. He was looking at doing more time in prison and had reached the end of the line. Radd had hit bottom.

I remember the first time I saw Radd in my courtroom. He was dressed in an orange jump suit and in chains. He looked broken. He *was* broken. He pled guilty and was brought into drug court. Radd was facing two years in prison if he didn't make it through drug court. The amount of prison time didn't make any difference to him at this point in his life. Radd wanted sobriety. He was determined to change.

Radd was serious about his recovery. He had a few bumps initially in drug court, but otherwise he did great. One Monday Radd appeared in front of me and announced that he'd gotten a job at a local nursery. It was the first real job he had in years!

He became a trusted employee for the nursery. It is difficult for our drug court participants to get full time employment because of the number of hours required in the program for treatment, counseling and various classes. Radd was able to work over thirty hours per week and for the first time in his life he qualified for benefits. When he became eligible for paid vacation, he was speechless. He had a hard time believing that he would actually get paid for a week he didn't work!

While in drug court, Radd committed his life to Jesus and was baptized. There is a Celebrate Recovery group at a church in Forest Grove, Oregon that a lot of our participants attend. The pastor of that church is a great supporter of drug court and has spoken at numerous drug court graduations. He often delivers a short gospel message, and Radd's graduation was no exception. Jesus has been a part of many drug court graduations in this way.

After Radd graduated from drug court, I invited him to speak at a county bar association meeting. The bar association meets monthly at a local restaurant. As the Presiding Judge for the Washington County Circuit Court, I presented a "State of the Court" speech at each January meeting. I always included an update on drug court. This time I wanted a drug court graduate to talk about his experience. Radd gave his testimony to the group of lawyers and judges. After he spoke, there was hardly a dry eye in the crowd.

Radd had a child born shortly after his graduation. There were serious complications and his young son died within a week after birth. It is with sadness that I mention Radd relapsed after this and found himself in the criminal justice system once again. I have hope that Radd will be able to recover his sobriety again and lead the life Jesus has planned for him. Radd's story is powerful and God will use it to His glory.

None of us is perfect. We all stumble. Lawyers, judges, doctors, plumbers, pastors, business men and women, moms and dads and drug court participants. We all make mistakes. I thank God for His grace and mercy every day.

> "But because of his great love for us, God, who is rich in mercy, made us alive with Christ even when we were dead in transgressions-it is by grace you have been saved. And God raised us up with Christ and seated us with him in the heavenly realms in Christ Jesus, in order that in the coming ages he might show the incomparable riches of his grace, expressed in his kindness to us in Christ Jesus.

For it is by grace you have been saved, through faith-and this is not from yourselves, it is the gift of God-not by works, so that no one can boast."
Ephesians 2:4-9

CHAPTER 19
THE CLUB

In the spring of 2006, I was asked to participate in a conference that was going to address the issues involved between the media (television, radio and newsprint) and the courts. Generally, there is tension between the public's right to know about a case being prosecuted and the defendant's right to a fair trial. In attendance were police, prosecutors, judges, defense attorneys and representatives from television, radio and the newsprint. The purpose of the conference was to identify the various conflicting interests and to explore how those could be resolved.

The format was informal. Everyone was given freedom to openly discuss the problems and to propose reasonable resolutions to the issues that were before us.

At the noon break we had a guest speaker. She was a member of an organization called Parents of Murdered Children (POMC). I had never heard of that organization before. She gave some background about POMC and then told her story about the loss of her child.

One thing she mentioned, that I will never forget, is how the word "murder" now has an entirely more profound effect on her. She stated that our society has desensitized the word "murder." There is an insensitivity toward murder that is inexplicable, she said. We see this attitude on TV, in movies, in books, in dinner theaters, and in video games.

As I was sitting in the room listening to her story I had a visceral reaction to her words that was totally unexpected. I became physically sick to my stomach. I didn't vomit, but I came close.

I did not want to become a member of this "club."

She explained that the POMC is a national organization with its principal office located in Cincinnati, Ohio.[6] Membership in POMC is open to those who have been cruelly bereaved by the murder of their child, family member or other loved one. Professionals who are involved in counseling family members are also allowed to join the organization. As stated on its website, POMC has no religious creed or affiliation.[7] The purpose of POMC is to provide support and assistance to the families of homicide victims. POMC also is working to reduce the crime of murder in any way they can.

I could sense that most of the other people in the room had similar feelings. You could see it on their faces. When she was finished I was so grateful that I was not eligible to be a member of POMC. Although there was an opportunity to speak with her after the meeting, I chose not to.

In the span of a few short months, I had become eligible for membership. Megan was murdered. I went to the POMC website, contacted someone from national headquarters and planned to attend the next local chapter meeting in Portland. It seemed so surreal to

---

6   National Organization of Parents Of Murdered Children, Inc. (POMC),www.pomc.com

7   see 6 above

me. The idea of attending a meeting that was solely centered on the common bond of a murdered child was almost unimaginable.

I was still crying buckets of tears during that time. I had no idea that:

> Those who sow in tears
>> will reap with songs of joy.
> He who goes out weeping,
>> carrying seed to sow,
> will return with songs of joy,
>> carrying sheaves with him.
>
>> Psalm 126:5-6

It was a cold, rainy night in Portland as Julie and I drove to our first POMC meeting. The meeting was located in an old Victorian style home in north Portland. We were a little early, so we stayed in our car for a while and prayed.

We saw some people going into the house. We gathered our courage and decided to go in also. It was a dark and dreary setting inside and out. As we entered the home we met a few people, all strangers to us. There were some snacks and coffee and tea in the kitchen. We mentioned that we had suffered a recent loss and were there to find out more about POMC. I did not tell anyone that I was the Presiding Judge for Washington County. Portland is in Multnomah County.

We were just there to listen.

The meeting began with introductions. People stated their names and how long they had been coming to POMC meetings. Some had been attending for more than twelve years. Others were more recent. One woman had been coming for a little less than a year. Each person told their story and shared their grief. I recognized the name of the woman who had been coming for less than a year. Her son had been shot and killed by a Washington County deputy earlier in the year. She was obviously devastated and in a very fragile condition. Whenever there is a police shooting, the county district attorney's office investigates the incident. Most of the time a grand jury is convened during the investigation. The shooting of her son was investigated and the grand jury concluded that the shooting was justified. The mom could not accept that conclusion. She was suffering and was extremely bitter. She had retained a lawyer and was going to pursue a claim against the sheriff's office and the county. She believed that the officer was not justified in using lethal force.[8]

Others at the meeting spoke of their tremendous losses also. Julie and I sensed a deep absence of hope for many of the people there. On one hand I saw an opportunity to share with them the hope of Jesus Christ. On the other hand, I knew that my role as Presiding Judge in Washington County was going to make if difficult to share my loss with those in attendance. They did not know my profession. Megan's case was still open. The authorities had not made an arrest yet. I did not want to jeopardize the ongoing investigation. Because of my position in the criminal justice system as a judge, it became clear that it was not appropriate for me to become involved with the POMC.

I have often wondered if God wanted me to share His gospel with those at that meeting. I don't know whether I made the right decision or not. Since then, God has given me the privilege to share the good news and the hope of Jesus with hundreds. My prayer every day is that God will give me the eyes to see and the ears to hear opportunities to share His love with the lost souls that He puts in my path.

---

8   A lawsuit was filed in federal court in Portland. The case was tried to a jury. The jury found the shooting was not justified and awarded damages to the family.

Julie and I decided that for the foreseeable future we would not be attending any more POMC meetings. Our hearts grieved for those people at that meeting. The losses they suffered could only be truly healed through the Great Physician. POMC is a wonderful organization that provides an outlet and an ear to the needs of the families of homicide victims. We receive a thoughtful remembrance card from POMC every year on the anniversary date of Megan's murder. It means a lot to us.

CHAPTER 20
HOSPITAL VISITS

A few years before Megan made her business cards, she developed a set of rules to live by. She called them "Meghan's rools." Here they are as she wrote them:

"do not mess with my clocks.
be nice.

no belching.
do not play my
barbes an less I say.

have fun.

do not play with
my brother an less
we want to look for
salamanders or play
tag. do not step on
my poste or rip it.

do not egnor
me and I wont
egnor you.

do not mess
up my bed."⁹

Megan was seven years old when she made up these rules. She was Daddy's little girl. I always looked forward to coming home after a long day at my law office to see her bright smiling face.

One time I got a frantic call from her mother. Megan was on the way to the hospital. She had tumbled down a hill at school and the ambulance was taking her to St. Vincent Hospital. I couldn't get to the hospital soon enough. When I arrived there, Megan was in the emergency room. As I walked into her room, I could see that her arm was broken and the doctor was preparing to set the break. Megan and I both cried when we saw each other. I was relieved to know that she was going to be okay.

As I also mentioned earlier, Megan was a horse lover. We had a pony that we kept in our large back yard. I built a stable and corral for it. A pony in a residential neighborhood didn't sit well with neighbors, so eventually we sold it.

Some time later we bought two horses. They were cutters. They were quick and could turn on a dime. Megan loved to ride them. The horses were stabled about a mile from where we lived...a much better arrangement than our back yard!

One day Zac, his mom and I were in Camas, Washington visiting some old friends. Camas is just across the Columbia River from Portland. On our way home, I received a call from a stranger on my cell phone. He told me that Megan had been taken to St. Vincent Hospital by ambulance on a backboard. He went on to explain that while Megan was riding a horse, it tripped, fell to the ground and rolled over her. He immediately called 911. The extent

---

9   See Appendix C

of Megan's injuries was unknown. To this day, I have no idea who the caller was.

I floored the gas pedal as we sped down Interstate 5 to St. Vincent Hospital. Zac and his mom were more than a little frightened as I broke every speed limit on the way!

After we reached the hospital, it took a few minutes to locate the area where Megan was being treated. We were led to the radiology department. Megan was undergoing some tests. She had been asking for me and I was allowed to go back to her. Once again another tearful reunion at a hospital. I will never forget her words, "Daddy, Daddy." Only parents can appreciate the wonderful sound of those words.

The doctors were concerned about potential neck and back injuries, but all the tests came back negative. Megan was not supposed to be riding the horse while we were gone. She was sorry. As we drove home a sense of comfort and relief filled me once again.

But those questions that I had before, "Was I a good parent?", "Could I protect her?", continued to haunt me.

But Megan was safe.

CHAPTER 21
SCOTT

Megan's murder occurred in Gladstone, Oregon which is in Clackamas County. The major crimes team for the county began the investigation immediately. Bob Maple from the Gladstone Police Department, Luke Streight from the Milwaukie Police Department and Scott Sudaisar from the Oregon Department of State Police were heading the team.

Senior Deputy District Attorney, Scott Healy, was assigned to investigate and prosecute Megan's case. Scott had plenty of experience in this area of criminal law. He had successfully prosecuted several high profile murder cases in Clackamas County. He was well suited for the task at hand.

I didn't contact Scott at the beginning of the investigation. I was aware of, and concerned about, the potential appearance of undue influence and conflict that the presiding judge of a neighboring county could have in this situation. Getting involved in any way could jeopardize the investigation and the ultimate outcome. My intent was to remain as far away as possible from the investigation and prosecution of this case. In spite of this, the defense attorney for the man who murdered my child tried to raise this very issue at the trial. More on this later.

Scott telephoned me at my office several months after he was assigned to the case. He met with Julie and me at our home to give us an update on the investigation. As we knew, Megan had been involved with some very bad people in the last couple years of her life. She had been selling drugs for one or more of her dealers. At the time of our first meeting, Scott told us that there were many "people of interest" who needed to be interviewed. Quite a few of them were presently located in the Washington County jail. His investigators were looking under every stone. There was much work to do.

At the conclusion of our first meeting with Scott, we exchanged contact information with each other. I felt that Scott was the perfect person to be assigned to Megan's case. I could already feel the hand of God working to bring her murderer to justice. Although Scott didn't know it at the time, I believed he was going to be working hand in hand with God.

This was our prayer.

"The Lord works righteousness and justice for all the oppressed." Psalm 103:6.

We knew that justice would prevail in the end. I was praying for the repentance and salvation of the one who took the life of my daughter. Oddly, I had no bitterness or anger toward this person. God had begun to weave the threads of forgiveness into my heart.

"For nothing is impossible with God." Luke 1:37

I later learned that there were many defendants in the Washington County jail who were interviewed. I never knew who they were because the investigators kept that information from me. A major portion of my responsibility as the presiding judge was sentencing many of the criminal population in our jail.

Our district attorney's office was making sure that I didn't sentence any of the potential witnesses in the case. Most of them were diverted from my courtroom without me ever knowing. However there were three defendants who slipped through the crack. One of them eventually became a major witness in Megan's murder trial.

CHAPTER 22
BUSTED

In May of 2006, about two months before Megan's murder, I was informed by the Portland police that Megan had been arrested and charged with delivery and possession of illegal drugs. Police found a substantial quantity of methamphetamine, cocaine and ecstasy in her car at the time of her arrest.

To most parents this arrest would be devastating news. To Julie and me this was an answer to prayer. I knew this arrest meant that eventually Megan would have to be accountable to a probation officer and a judge. I was hopeful that she would be allowed to participate in a drug court program.

There was hope...this was an answer to prayer.

Some parents are fortunate enough to have this prayer answered. On one occasion, I was sentencing a young man who pled guilty to possession and delivery of heroin. The prosecutor laid out the facts of the case and it was apparent that the defendant was an addict. The courtroom was crowded. In the back I noticed a man and woman who were obviously interested in the case. I asked the defendant if his parents were in the courtroom. He said they were. After the sentencing I had one of my staff get the attention of the parents. I wanted to speak with them in my chambers. I stepped off the bench and waited for them to come back to my office.

As they were coming into my chambers I had them take a seat. This was their son's first conviction. They were afraid of the path their son had chosen. Although it was hard for them, they were relieved that he was now in the criminal justice system. I told them about Megan and her addiction and her murder. They were shocked. They were also Christians. We talked about addiction, its consequences and about God's saving grace. I was able to comfort them with the same comfort I received from God. Before we ended our conversation I prayed for them and their son. We all cried together. This scenario is not unusual. God has given me many opportunities to pray with moms and dads in my chambers. I seize that opportunity whenever I can.

Megan obtained a lawyer in the drug case. I learned later that the lawyer negotiated a plea bargain with the Multnomah County District Attorney's office. The plea agreement would allow Megan to receive a misdemeanor conviction rather than a felony. As it turned out, Megan was murdered before she had an opportunity to plea to the misdemeanor.

I have wondered since then what her drug dealer thought of that plea bargain. Did he believe Megan was going to rat on him?

CHAPTER 23
BLUE HAIR

Have you ever made a promise to someone and then regretted it? Let me tell you about one that I made in open court and on the record during a drug court session. Brittany was one of our participants who was really struggling in the beginning of her program. She was facing several years in prison if she didn't complete drug court. She was a mom. She had no contact with her daughter for years. Heroin was her drug of choice.

She was usually nervous when she appeared in front of me on Mondays. It was difficult to establish any type of rapport with her. Eventually she began to settle down and find her way through drug court and the recovery process. As I mentioned earlier, one of the requirements of drug court is to obtain employment. For some people this is very difficult. There are times when we encourage a participant to attend a trade school or a community college if it seems appropriate. In Brittany's case she wanted to go to beauty school. It seemed like a good choice for her. After all, her hair was a different color every couple of months!

Brittany was able to get some financial aid and start beauty school. However, there were times when she still seemed to be struggling in her recovery and in her drug court obligations.

One Monday when Brittany was before me for her weekly status check, I felt that she needed to have some additional motivation. Recently she had made contact with her estranged daughter. She had a lot of damage to repair in that relationship. She seemed to be overwhelmed. So I said, "Brittany, if you graduate from drug court, I will let you dye my hair any color you want." Where did those words come from? Was the Holy Spirit behind this? Does the Holy Spirit really have a sense of humor? The words were out of my mouth before I thought of the consequences.

That promise was made in front of a courtroom full of drug court participants, spectators and drug court staff. Brittany's demeanor changed immediately. She said, "Judge, I am going to graduate!" There was no doubt in my mind that soon my gray hair would be transformed into a flaming red, a royal blue or a dazzling purple color!

The Washington County courthouse system has four separate sites. My promise spread quickly from building to building, from department to department. Meanwhile, as the weeks rolled by, Brittany was doing great. She was motivated. She was doing excellent in school and embracing her recovery. She was a new person.

The promise became a topic of discussion at our weekly staffing meetings as Brittany rapidly and steadily progressed through the program. As she was entering the last phase of drug court, one of our staffing members decided to contact the local newspaper. A decision was made by the paper to cover the event.

Brittany sailed through the final phase of drug court and a date for her graduation was set. It was decided *by others* that the coloring of my hair would be part of her graduation ceremony.

The courtroom was full on the day of Brittany's graduation. Her mother and daughter were in attendance. Fellow workers from the courthouse were there. Most of them had never been to a graduation before. None of them had ever seen a presiding judge get a dye job.

The newspaper reporter and photographer came early. We had decided to color my hair back in the jury room, where staffing takes place. Brittany allowed me to choose my own color. I chose royal blue, the color of my alma mater, the University of Kentucky.

Back in the jury room, Brittany laid out all the tools of her trade on the table. Most of the staffing team, the reporter and the photographer gathered around as Brittany began to work. It took about thirty minutes. She even did my mustache and soul patch. It would have looked really weird if she didn't. At least that's what she said!

When she finished, it was time to go out on the bench for our regular drug court session followed by the graduation. I had to walk through the courtroom to get to my chambers. The walk through the courtroom was one of the most uncomfortable walks in my life. There was some laughter, some noises that are hard to describe and some stares that I will never forget. There were also many photo opportunities...even some deputies took pictures.

I went through the regular drug court session. One statement from a drug court participant as he appeared before me was "It's hard to take you seriously, Judge." I knew at that time there was no way the blue hair would last longer than one evening.

I never promised how long I would keep it blue!

In spite of my blue hair, Brittany's graduation was the main thing. It was one of the best graduations in drug court, ever. She had come into drug court as a caterpillar and emerged a butterfly. She was reunited with her mother and her daughter.

After court was over that day, I slipped through a side door of the courthouse with a baseball hat covering my head!

Julie was also at the graduation. As she was leaving the courthouse, she ran into one of Brittany's instructors from the beauty college. She happened to have a conversation about how to remove the coloring from my hair. Julie purchased the recommended chemical on her way home. She had some things to do that evening, so she left me some additional written instructions on how to remove the dye.

When I arrived home that evening, I looked on the kitchen counter and saw the "do it yourself" dye removal package and the written instructions from Julie. I was thrilled that I didn't have to shave my head that night. The package of chemicals had some instructions on it. I read them, eager to start the process. I felt like I was back in my high school chemistry lab again as I combined several chemicals in a plastic bottle at the kitchen sink.

I then went upstairs to the bathroom to put the solution in my hair. It was supposed to remain in my hair for about twenty minutes. I wrapped a towel around my head, went back downstairs to the kitchen and put the plastic bottle in the trash can below the sink. And then the pain began. The top of my head felt like it was on fire. I ran back upstairs again and into the shower. The blue was coming out!

Although painful, the chemical removal of the blue dye was a success. I went back down to the kitchen. I was curious about the plastic bottle that I put in the trash can. I pulled it out. It had actually gotten bigger. I decided to twist off the top. This was a mistake. As I was opening the lid, the bottle exploded all over the kitchen. I spent the next hour cleaning up the mess. When Julie came home that evening, she just smiled, sort of! The bleach stains remain to this day.

The next day at the courthouse, several people came by to see how I was doing. At least, that was their purported motive. My hair was now beach-boy blonde! But the blue was gone! Thankfully.

There was a full page article with color pictures in the local newspaper later that week. The title of the article read "Drug Court Judge Gets the Blues."

CHAPTER 24
A DRUG COURT GRADUATION

A drug court graduation is a joyous event. Graduations always happen on Mondays immediately following our regular drug court session. The Beaverton Bakery cakes are decorated individually for each graduate. The graduate gets to pick the flavor of cake he or she wants. My favorite is chocolate. I try to encourage our graduates to choose chocolate. Sometimes it works, other times not.

The courtroom is decorated with festive colors. We have balloons, colorful tablecloths and punch. The courtroom is transformed into a party room in celebration of the graduate. Some of the graduates have never had a party in their honor, not even a birthday party.

At the beginning of a graduation ceremony, members of the staffing team come up to the podium to talk about the graduate. Usually the people speaking are the ones who have had a close relationship with the graduate. Often members of the family speak. There have been many occasions when there was hardly a dry eye in the courtroom after a mom or dad had talked about how grateful they were for their son or daughter's remarkable turnaround.

We have established a unique ceremony. A paper shredder is brought into the courtroom for each graduation. Copies of the charging documents are given to the graduate by the district attorney. Page by page and with a huge smile, the graduate shreds his or her charges in the shredder. Each time there is a deafening round of applause as the charging document is shredded. The prison time has been symbolically nullified!

The deputy district attorney also creates a poster board of booking pictures for each participant. Many of the participants have numerous booking photos. The photos are generally not very flattering. Usually you can see the gruesome physical effects that drug abuse has caused over time in each of the photos. In the middle of the poster board is a recent photo of the graduate with a big smile. The contrast is often breathtaking.

Our elected district attorney, Robert Hermann, speaks at almost every graduation. Without his support and endorsement, our drug court would not be in existence. His office makes the final call on who can enter drug court.

I speak last at each graduation. I tell how long the graduate has been in drug court and how many clean days have been accumulated. I reiterate the mission of drug court which is to change people's lives, to break the cycle of addiction, to reunite families and to promote community safety.

In every graduation the mission statement of drug court has been accomplished. However, this does not always ensure that the graduate will not suffer a setback. Drug court has its share of graduate relapses. This is not unexpected, however each graduate has been given the necessary tools to deal with relapse during his or her time in drug court. Each has a relapse plan. Most of the relapses have resulted in successful efforts to recapture clean and sober lifestyles.

I then give the graduate a Washington County Adult Drug Court Certificate of Graduation. The certificate is in a very handsome glass frame and is sequentially numbered.

Lastly I give the graduating participant a skeleton key. Megan collected skeleton keys. The keys are old and sometimes rusty. I search for these keys around town and usually find them in local antique shops. In fact, when I go into some of the local shops the salesperson knows why I'm there. "Here comes Judge Kohl for his skeleton keys!"

As I give the skeleton key to the graduate at the end of the ceremony, I relate that when a person is born into this world there are many doors that are open to him or her. Doors of family opportunity, doors of social opportunity, doors of employment opportunity and doors of educational opportunity. As a person becomes more involved in drug use, abuse and addiction, the doors start to close, one by one. Eventually all the doors are closed. As a person begins to recover from drug addiction, the doors start to open once again.

The skeleton key, I explain, represents the graduate's recovery. Recovery has begun to open doors that had been previously closed. Most of all, the door of rebuilding family relationships has been opened. We see this phenomenon at almost every graduation where moms and dads are welcoming back the prodigal son or daughter... where sons and daughters are welcoming back the lost mom or dad... and where brothers and sisters are reestablishing their relationships.

Near the end of the graduation, the graduate has an opportunity to speak. Most graduates are so overcome with emotion that they can get only a few words out. Others have been extremely eloquent. Sometimes letters from family members who cannot be present are read at the graduation.[10] Oftentimes, I receive letters from recent graduates which are read in open court as an encouragement to the participants.[11]

At the end of the graduation, we eat cake and drink punch together; counselors, mentors, fellow participants, moms, dads, sons,

---

10   See Appendix D
11   See Appendix E

daughters, brothers, sisters, defense attorney, district attorney, deputy sheriff, probation officers and judge. This is a time to celebrate and socialize with the participants, their friends and relatives. Outside of drug court, you don't see prosecutors, defense attorneys, probation officers, police, judges and defendants sharing a piece of cake and having every day normal conversations centered around a joyful event.

I have seen some attorneys come into my courtroom during this part of graduation and leave with very puzzled looks on their faces. One time a deputy sheriff approached me after a drug court session. He had worked in the courthouse for years. He told me the difference between drug court and other courtrooms was the laughter and smiles that he saw coming from the participants' faces.

From hopeless to triumphant!

CHAPTER 25
THE ARREST

During the spring of 2007, I was informed by law enforcement authorities that they had narrowed the investigation to a particular suspect. Robert Burton Bettelyoun.

On June 1, 2007, I received the news that we had been praying for since the murder. Detective Maple from the Gladstone Police Department called me on my cell phone while I was on my way to work that morning.

He told me that Robert Bettelyoun had just been arrested in Vancouver, Washington. It was a Friday. They were going to interrogate him over the weekend and he would be arraigned on Monday, June 4, in the Clackamas County Circuit Court. Robert was being charged with two counts of Aggravated Murder and one count of Robbery in the First Degree.

Overwhelmed with emotion, tears were streaming from my eyes. I called Julie to let her know. My mind was reeling with the news of the arrest. We only live a few miles from the courthouse but I don't remember the rest of the drive there. I was able to get through the day only with the help of Jesus. The waves of grief and sorrow began to flood anew.

How could I have managed without Him?

Once again the news media was all over the story. I refused to return their phone calls, and thankfully they didn't press me for any statements. I felt like the media was at least respecting my desire for privacy.

The name of the suspect sounded familiar to me, so I checked our Washington County criminal records. It happened that Robert had appeared in front of me several years earlier on a felony charge. He'd pled guilty to a charge of Criminal Mischief in the First Degree and I sentenced him to probation. It was an uneventful sentencing as far as I could tell. He was only in front of me for less than five minutes.

Robert was arraigned in Clackamas County Circuit Court on June 4, 2007 and officially charged with two counts of Aggravated Murder and one count of Robbery in the First Degree. The aggravated murder counts carried the possibility of the death sentence, life without parole or life with the possibility of parole after serving thirty years in prison. The robbery charge carried a penalty of ninety months in prison.

Count One alleged a murder committed during the course of a robbery, and Count Two alleged a murder for hire. At Robert's initial appearance bail was denied. He was to remain in the custody of the Clackamas County Sheriff until the final disposition of the case.

After several appearances in front of different judges, the case was finally scheduled for trial on June 2, 2008. I was not hopeful that the trial would happen on that date. Most murder trials languish in the system longer than that. I knew the system. I knew there would be numerous hearings that would take place over the next year or so. I knew that there would be a time of waiting. I was willing to wait.

"I waited patiently for the Lord;
He turned to me and heard my cry.

He lifted me out of the slimy pit,
    out of the mud and mire.
He set my feet on a rock
    and gave me a firm place to stand.
He put a new song in my mouth,
    a hymn of praise to our God.
Many will see and fear
    and put their trust in the LORD."

Psalm 40:1-3

I had complete confidence in the district attorney who was assigned to the case. As I mentioned earlier, his name was Scott Healy. He was experienced in trying murder cases. He had never lost a murder trial.

And there was no way he was going to lose this one.

I learned from Scott that he kept a blown-up picture of Megan in his office from the beginning of the investigation until the end of the trial. Scott was passionate about bringing the murderer of Megan to justice and was fully invested!

Chapter 26
More Comfort

God has given me many opportunities to pray with drug court participants, victims and relatives of victims. For example, in Oregon, victims have the right to appear at every stage of a criminal proceeding including the sentencing. Sometimes I see that God has led a victim to be healed by the forgiveness that only God can offer. You can see it and hear it in the voice and words of the victim as he or she is speaking at the sentencing.

Other times I see victims who have not forgiven and have become bitter because of the crime committed by the defendant. They are upset and angry at the criminal justice system because the consequences are not as severe as they'd hoped for. In some of these cases I ask staff to tell the victims that I would like to speak with them in my office. When they come into my office, I have them sit down and ask them to tell me more about their situation.

In one case the victims' house had been broken into by the defendant and some family jewelry had been taken and sold by the defendant. The defendant was a meth addict. The jewelry was not recovered. The victims thought the defendant should be sentenced to prison for a long time. They were extremely angry.

They came back to my chambers. I then told them about Megan and what happened to her. Their loss, I explained, was only property. And then I told them about drug court and how addicts' lives are being changed. I tried to give them a different perspective about the drug addict. There were a few questions and then I asked them if I could pray for them. Somewhat surprised, they said yes and I prayed for God to heal their anger and bitterness and to give them a forgiving heart. The victims were moved.

Thank you God for giving me these precious opportunities to share Your goodness.

On another occasion a defendant appeared in front of me for sentencing on two counts of Manslaughter in the Second Degree. Each count carried a mandatory sentence of seventy-five months which meant a possibility of one hundred fifty months in prison if served consecutively.

In Oregon, this is considered a Measure 11 crime. Measure 11 crimes carry determinate sentences. This means that if a defendant is sentenced to one hundred fifty months in prison, then that is the actual sentence he or she will serve. There is no time off for good behavior. It is a day for day sentence. It is considered "truth in sentencing."

However, the defendant's attorney and the district attorney worked out a deal to allow a sentence of seventy-five months total. This meant that the sentences would be served concurrently rather than consecutively. The parents agreed to this arrangement.

At the sentencing, the district attorney related the facts of the case. The defendant had been operating a car while intoxicated. He had a male friend, Jim (not his real name) in the back seat of his car and Jim's girlfriend, Sue (not her real name) in the passenger seat. They had just picked up Sue from her apartment. It was early in the morning. As the defendant was speeding down a residential street he crashed into a rock retaining wall. The crash was so loud it woke people throughout the entire neighborhood.

Police and ambulance personnel arrived at the scene shortly after the crash. Sue was killed instantly and Jim died on the way to the hospital. The police located the driver of the vehicle on the roof of the house next to the crash scene. The force of the impact was so great that the defendant had been ejected from the car and onto the roof. He was unconscious. They did not expect him to survive. But he did.

He was released from the hospital about three months later. He was charged with the manslaughter counts and remained in jail until the date of his sentencing.

After the district attorney concluded his portion of the sentencing, the parents of Jim and Sue were asked if they would like to say anything. The parents chose not to. I could see they were hurting. The courtroom was packed with people, but you could still hear a pin drop.

Before I sentenced the defendant I asked him if he had anything to say. He turned and looked at the parents and said he was sorry. I sentenced him to the agreed upon term of seventy-five months in prison. I wanted to speak with the parents. They were willing to come back.

I took a break from the bench and walked into my chambers. The parents were seated around my desk. I thanked them for agreeing to speak with me. I told them that I knew the extent of pain, grief and sorrow that they were experiencing. I could tell that they were thinking, "No you don't." Through tears, I told them about the murder of my daughter, Megan. They knew then that I could speak of the pain and suffering of losing a child.

The parents broke down sobbing. I told them how Jesus had comforted me during this loss and how only Jesus could have given me the power to forgive my daughter's murderer. I could not have done that on my own. It was only by the power of the Holy Spirit. The same Holy Spirit that raised Jesus from the grave was in me. We talked for about thirty minutes. There were many tears.

They shared more about the hopes and dreams they had for their children. I mentioned that I attended Solid Rock Church. They told me that Jim and Sue had attended the Friday evening services for college age kids at Solid Rock. At the end of our time together I prayed for them.

Each time God blesses me with these divine appointments to help comfort others, I am reminded of the Shepherd's psalm:

The LORD is my shepherd, I shall not be in want.
He makes me lie down in green pastures,
he leads me beside quiet waters,
he restores my soul.
He guides me in paths of righteousness
for His name's sake.
Even though I walk
through the valley of the shadow of death,
I will fear no evil,
for you are with me;
Your rod and your staff,
they comfort me.

You prepare a table before me
in the presence of my enemies.
You anoint my head with oil;
my cup overflows.
Surely goodness and love will follow me
all the days of my life,
and I will dwell in the house of the LORD,
forever. Psalm 23

And again, 2 Corinthians 1:3-4 is the most meaningful scripture to me when I have the opportunity to share God's healing comfort with victims of crimes and other tragedies:

"Praise be to the God and Father of our Lord Jesus Christ, the Father of compassion and the God of all comfort, who comforts us in all our troubles, so that we can comfort those in any trouble with the comfort we ourselves have received from God."

CHAPTER 27
THE TRIAL BEGINS

The trial of the State of Oregon v. Robert B. Bettelyoun was scheduled to begin with jury selection on February 2, 2009, and was expected to take about six weeks. The marriage of my stepdaughter was set for March 7, 2009. Joy and sorrow were headed for a collision. Only through the faithful prayer support of our church family and many others were Julie and I able to experience the peace that goes beyond all understanding during this storm.

"And the peace of God, which transcends all understanding, will guard your hearts and your minds in Christ Jesus." Philippians 4:7.

Going through the aggravated murder trial of my daughter and the events leading up to the marriage of my stepdaughter during the same time was a huge contrast. On one hand, seeing the joy in the face of my wife and her daughter was indescribable. On the other hand, the sorrow I was experiencing during the trial was just as indescribable.

Joy and sorrow were crashing into one another. God was teaching me that joy and sorrow can walk hand in hand, but only through the power of Jesus. Paul said in 2 Corinthians 6:4-10 that:

> ...as servants of God we commend ourselves in every way: in great endurance; in troubles, hardships and distresses; in beatings, imprisonment and riots;...and yet we live on; beaten, and yet not killed; SORROWFUL, YET ALWAYS REJOICING; poor, yet making many rich; having nothing, and yet possessing everything. (Emphasis added)

Sorrow is beautiful in her own way and joy is beautiful in his own way. One has the beauty of moonlight and the other has the beauty of the sun. Only Jesus can unite the two.

> Sorrow was beautiful, but her beauty was the beauty of the moonlight shining through the leafy branches of the trees in the wood, and making little pools of silver here and there on the soft green moss below.
>
> When Sorrow sang, her notes were like the low sweet call of the nightingale, and in her eyes was the unexpectant gaze of one who has ceased to look for coming gladness. She could weep in tender sympathy with those who weep, but to rejoice with those who rejoice was unknown to her.
>
> Joy was beautiful, too, but his was the radiant beauty of the summer morning. His eyes still held the glad laughter of childhood, and his hair had the glint of the sunshine's kiss. When Joy sang his voice soared upward as the lark's, and his step was the step of a conqueror who has never known defeat. He could rejoice with all who rejoice, but to weep with those who weep was unknown to him.
>
> "But we can never be united," said Sorrow wistfully.
>
> "No, never." And Joy's eyes shadowed as he spoke. "My path lies through the sunlit meadows,

the sweetest roses bloom for my gathering, and the blackbirds and thrushes await my coming to pour forth their most joyous lays."

"My path," said Sorrow, turning slowly away, "leads through the darkening woods; with moonflowers only shall my hands be filled. Yet the sweetest of all earth songs-the love song of the night-shall be mine; farewell, Joy, farewell."

Even as she spoke they became conscious of a form standing beside them; dimly seen, but of a kingly Presence, and great and holy awe stole over them as they sank on their knees before Him.

"I see Him as the King of Joy," whispered Sorrow, "for on His head are many crowns, and the nailprints in His hands and feet are the scars of a great victory. Before Him all my sorrow is melting away into deathless love and gladness, and I give myself to Him forever."

"Nay, Sorrow," said Joy softly, "but I see Him as the King of Sorrow, and the crown on His head is a crown of thorns, and the nailprints in His hands and feet are the scars of a great agony. I, too, give myself to Him forever, for sorrow with Him must be sweeter than any joy that I have known."

"Then we are ONE in Him," they cried in gladness, "for none but He could unite Joy and Sorrow."

Hand in hand they passed out into the world to follow Him through storm and sunshine, in the bleakness of winter cold and the warmth of summer gladness, "as sorrow yet always rejoicing."

From "Streams in the Desert" by Mrs. Charles E. Cowman, daily devotional
August 19.

I had made the decision that I was not going to attend the trial. Scott called me in the evenings to give me a daily update on the status of who was going to testify next and generally how the case was proceeding. As I mentioned earlier, the defense was trying to convince the jury that somehow the prosecution of the case was based, in part, on the fact that the father of the victim was the Presiding Judge in Washington County. I believed that my presence throughout the trial would become a distraction. I was not willing to take that chance. So Scott and I talked almost every night during the trial.

I had presided over hundreds of trials since taking the bench in 1997. I had seen the full range of trials from misdemeanor theft to murder by abuse. The workings of a trial were nothing new to me. The stages of a trial were the same in misdemeanors and felonies: selection of a jury, opening statements, presentation of the state's case in chief, the defendant's case, closing arguments, instructions of the court to the jury and then deliberation by the jury.

In the months leading up to the trial there were many hearings concerning evidence that the state was intending to use at trial. The defendant's attorneys were trying to keep the jury from hearing some of the state's evidence. They were unsuccessful in almost all their attempts to keep evidence from the jury.

In an aggravated murder trial there are two phases: the guilt stage and the sentencing stage. If the jury finds a defendant guilty of aggravated murder, the sentencing phase proceeds next. The jury hears evidence both from the state and from the defendant to determine which of three possible sentences should be imposed: life with the possibility of parole after thirty years, life without the possibility of parole or death by lethal injection.

Jury selection took two weeks. The lawyers questioned more than one hundred potential jurors. The final jury was selected on February 17, 2009. Opening statements were made to the jury on February 18, 2009. The trial had begun.

CHAPTER 28
GOD ANSWERS PRAYER

God answered a huge prayer for me in October of 2007. I had been praying to God that He would let me know where Megan was. I begged Him to allow me to give up my salvation for Megan if she was not with Him. This was a prayer that God had heard from me hundreds of times since July 21, 2006.

Not only was I willing to give up my salvation, but there were times when I thought about ending my own life. These were the very darkest of days immediately after the murder. These were the days where there was no hope, no desire to go forward, yet I was still going to work every day, still functioning in a somewhat normal manner, still on autopilot.

You either turn to God or you turn away from Him in storms like this. Most of the time I was turning to Him, but there were moments when I was not. God always found a way of turning me back.

"He restores my soul, He guides me in paths of righteousness for his name's sake." Psalm 23:3

God always restored my hope; He restored my soul.

On October 4, 2007, when I arrived home from work, Julie greeted me as usual with a hug and a kiss. She said, "Tom, sit down. I have something to show you." I knew something was up but had no idea how huge this "something" was going to be.

Julie said she was nervous about this and didn't quite know how to start. She told me that God had woken her up at 3:30 am and put "something" on her heart. She went to the computer and began to type words that were coming from the Holy Spirit. She was excited, anxious, unsure and nervous.

Julie left the room and came back with a sheet of paper in her hand and gave it to me. On the sheet of paper was the message she received from God at 3:30 in the morning on October 4, 2007. It read:

Now I lay me down to sleep
You prayed the Lord my soul would keep

I died too young, is what they say
Yet now I know the one true Way

Jesus died for me, my soul to save
There is no more pain beyond this grave

From the tormentor, God has set me free
Now I worship Christ on bended knee

He walks with me, right by my side
With Him in Heaven, I now reside

We will meet again, I can promise you such
For God is faithful, true and just

So rejoice with me through the tears you weep
For now my soul is His to keep.

Meagan's Reassurance
Given to us from God
October 4, 2007, 3:30 am

I was overwhelmed. I wept tears of joy. Julie and I embraced. I had never told Julie about my prayer time with Megan when she was a little girl; that I would pray "Now I lay me down to sleep..."

God answers prayers. He answers them in His time and in His way, but He always answers prayers. Not some of the time, not most of the time, but all of the time.

"And we know that in all things God works for the good of those who love him, who have been called according to his purpose." Romans 8:28

As Jesus hung on the cross at Golgotha, one criminal on his right and one on his left, the Roman soldiers came up to him and mocked him:

> "...'If you are the king of the Jews, save yourself.'... One of the criminals who hung there hurled insults at him: 'Aren't you the Christ? Save yourself and us!' But the other criminal rebuked him. 'Don't you fear God,' he said, 'since you are under the same sentence? We are punished justly, for we are getting what our deeds deserve. But this man has done nothing wrong.'
>
> Then he said, 'Jesus, remember me when you come into your kingdom.' Jesus answered him, 'I tell you the truth, today you will be with me in paradise." Luke 23:37-43

At the end of her life, God gave Megan one more chance to spend eternity with Him. I believe she accepted, just like the thief on the cross who was saved at the last second.

Megan is spending eternity with Jesus. We don't know much about the thief on the cross. We do know that he was not baptized, didn't belong to any group of believers and didn't have a clue about salvation before he acknowledged Jesus as Lord and Savior. But we do know that he is spending eternity with Jesus because Jesus said he would! God is the God of second, third and scores of chances. For Jeri and Radd and for Megan.

Now THAT is hope!

CHAPTER 29
THE VERDICT

The evidentiary portion of the trial, State v. Robert Burton Bettelyoun, began on February 19, 2009. Intercessory prayers from friends, family and our church community began in earnest on that day. We were asking for prayer support for the DA, the judge, the jury and for Teresa and Zac, for our marriage, for the very soul of Robert Bettelyoun and that justice would come surely and swiftly. We were camping out in Philippians 4:6-7:

> "Do not be anxious about anything, but in everything, by prayer and petition, with thanksgiving, present your request to God. And the peace of God, which transcends all understanding, will guard your hearts and your minds in Christ Jesus."

When Scott and I talked, he never mentioned any doubt about the outcome. He was always upbeat. Scott spent hundreds of hours in preparation for this trial, the picture of Megan in his office fueling his fire. It served to remind him of the beautiful young woman whose life was brutally ended by this senseless crime.

The state concluded their case several weeks into the trial and the defense was ready to begin their case on March 10. Scott thought the defense would take two or three days, but it took longer than expected. We received word that closing arguments were scheduled for March 25. Scott thought the case was going extremely well. He expressed that he sensed a different sort of atmosphere in the courtroom than in past trials. We knew it was the prayers of the intercessors who were making the difference; in the courtroom and on the home front.

On March 25, 2009, Julie and I were in the courtroom as closing arguments were scheduled to begin. This was our first appearance at trial. We sat near the front. Robert Bettelyoun had not been brought into the courtroom yet. We waited. And then we saw a door open. Robert came into the courtroom in leg chains and hand chains with two armed deputies at his side. He was dressed in a shirt and tie.

Robert and I glanced at each other. I had no idea how I was going to feel. It was surreal. The person who brutally murdered Megan was sitting within fifteen feet from me. He was talking with his lawyer. I was flooded with emotions. It was harder than I thought it would be. Just then, I felt the presence of God in my heart and all the emotions began to subside. I knew this was possible only through the work of the Holy Spirit. There was no hatred, no bitterness, no vindictiveness. There was only sorrow.

Closing arguments began, and for the first time I learned exactly how Megan was murdered. I had never asked. I really didn't want to know. What difference would it make?

I won't describe what happened here. No parent should ever have to hear the horrific details of how their child died.

Scott gave an excellent closing argument. The jury began deliberating later on that day.

We went home that evening. It was a difficult day. I knew that I had made the right decision about not attending the trial until then.

I received a phone call from Scott on March 26, 2009. The verdict was in. There were three counts that the jury needed to decide. The jury found the defendant not guilty of aggravated murder in the course of a robbery, guilty of aggravated murder for hire and guilty of robbery in the first degree. I felt relief with the verdict.

But no verdict could bring back Megan.

The next stage of the trial was to determine the sentence Robert was going to receive. For the robbery in the first degree count, Robert would be sentenced to ninety months in prison. For the aggravated murder conviction, the jury had three options: (1) life in prison with the possibility of parole after serving thirty years, (2) life with no possibility of parole or, (3) the death sentence.

The jury would make their decision after hearing evidence from the state and the defense in what is referred to as the "sentencing phase" of the trial. Scott told me that the sentencing phase was set to begin on April 1 and that Teresa, Zac and I would be testifying that morning. The state was seeking the death penalty and Robert's attorneys would be asking the jury to give him the least harsh punishment, life with the possibility of parole after serving thirty years. We were hoping and praying for life without the possibility of parole.

While there was some measure of relief with the verdict, and we were pleased that the truth overcame lies, we did not find joy in celebration, nor did the verdict indicate full victory in our eyes. Yes, victory here on earth, but spiritually we felt full victory would come with the defendant's admission, true repentance and sorrow, followed by a desire to make things right with God. Then the angels in heaven would have reason to rejoice and God would have victory over the devil. So we continued to pray for Robert.

We could see in the eyes of some people that they didn't understand our thinking. Some believed that Robert should "burn in hell." We did believe in a God of justice, and indeed Robert needed to pay the consequences of his actions here on earth. But we also believed that our God desires that none should perish eternally and that all would come to accept His mercy and grace and be redeemed.

"The Lord is not slow in keeping his promise, as some understand slowness. He is patient with you, not wanting anyone to perish, but everyone to come to repentance." 2 Peter 3:9

Robert's earthly destiny was in the hands of the jury, but his eternal destiny was up to him, he had a choice. God offers a way out. God offers hope. At this point, Robert was showing no remorse, no accountability.

Scott was coming over to our house on the evening of March 31 to prepare me for the next stage of the trial. God was also preparing my heart for something else.

CHAPTER 30
THE SENTENCE

April 1 was the day that Teresa, Zac and I were scheduled to testify in the sentencing phase of the trial. Scott had spent several hours at our house the night before in preparation for my testimony. Earlier in the day I had prepared an outline of what I wanted to say to the jury.

Julie and I drove over to Oregon City early in the morning on the 1st. We were so blessed to have the support of many friends and family praying for us that day. I was also blessed to have three friends from our drug court staffing team sitting with us in the courtroom; Duane Worley, Aaron Altstadt and Joy Arrington. Duane was a mentor, Aaron was the deputy sheriff and Joy was the probation officer assigned to the drug court staffing team. Their physical presence in the courtroom was so encouraging and comforting to me.

Teresa testified first. She testified as only a mother could, full of extreme and debilitating grief. She was completely broken.

Zac's testimony was powerful and impactful to the jury. I could see in their faces that they felt the pain and suffering that Zac expressed. He had been quiet in sharing his grief. But here, in the presence of the jury, he shared the raw impact of his sister's murder on his life; the total and devastating loss.

Zac told of the pain of having to wake his mother in the late hours of the night and deliver the message that her daughter had been murdered. No son should have to do that; no parent should have to hear that. His testimony was flowing to the jury through tears that had been held back for so long. Zac is a strong young man, full of integrity. I was so proud of how he expressed himself with brutal honesty and vulnerability.

I pray that he will be able to experience the healing that can only come through Jesus.

I testified next. In my role as a judge, I hear people testify every day from the witness stand. Now I was on the witness stand and would have given anything not to be in that position. Zac and Teresa had testified previously during the guilt phase of the trial, however this was the first time that the jury would hear from me.

It is hard to tell what the jury might have expected from me. I was the Presiding Judge from another county; the father of Megan, whom they had not heard from yet. I shared my heart with them. The heart of a father who had lost his little girl to the horror of a brutal murder. I shared the joy of the early years when Megan was growing up into the beautiful young woman that she would become. I shared the difficult times that followed the divorce and the difficult times that preceded her death.

I was also able to share the blessing and comfort that my church family had been to me through this difficult time. And then I spoke to the defendant directly through my tears that were flowing freely. I told him that I had forgiven him, that I held no animosity toward him and that I hoped one day that we could talk.

I told Robert that one day he will have to stand before the Ultimate Judge and that before that day, I hoped he would fall on his knees and ask for God's forgiveness. I told him the sobering truth: "You will spend eternity on one side or the other."

Up until that moment, I had not seen Robert show any emotion. It seemed like he had remained stone faced and indifferent. My guess is, he was that way throughout the trial. But as I was speaking directly to him, with the heart that God had prepared for me, Robert began to cry. We were looking at each other, face to face, man to man, and both of us were now weeping. When I finished my testimony, the judge asked the defense attorney if she had any questions for me. She did not.

The rest of the day was spent with the state presenting evidence urging that the death penalty was appropriate for Robert. That was the state's agenda. I was praying for life in prison.

Over the next two days the defense presented their evidence to show why Robert did not deserve the death penalty. The defense strategy was to bring in family members and friends to get sympathy from the jury. They even brought in his young daughter who pleaded with the jury to save his life.

On April 9, 2009, the jury returned their verdict of life in prison without the possibility of parole. The sentencing took place on the same day, immediately following the jury's verdict. Robert is now serving life without the possibility of parole at the Two Rivers Correctional Institution in Umatilla, Oregon.

The appeal of the verdict began immediately. It will take years for the appeal process to run its course.

In the meantime, I took comfort in the presence of the Lord, not yet knowing what else He had planned.

CHAPTER 31
FORGIVENESS

A year and a half later, in the fall of 2010, I felt God pressing on my heart to have a face-to-face meeting with Robert.

I was willing, but nervous..."to what end, God?"

I prayed about it. I had to trust God on this. So, in December of 2010, I wrote a letter to Robert. At our Friday morning men's group we prayed over the letter before it was mailed. Here it is:

"Dear Robert,

You probably didn't expect a letter from me. I have been praying about this for a long time, so I thought it was time to put prayer into action. As you know, I have forgiven you a long time ago. There is no hatred, no animosity and no bitterness. God has allowed this to take place.

I would like to visit you some time to talk. Not about the trial, but just to talk. If you would have it in your heart, I would greatly appreciate this opportunity.

Thanks for reading this.

I am in His grip always,

Tom Kohl"

Less than a week later, to my surprise...but not to God's!...I received a letter from Robert. He was willing to meet with me. He enclosed a visitor application with his response. As I was researching the application process I began to realize that arranging a meeting with him was not going to be easy. There were rules and regulations that governed this process.

The first obstacle was a general prohibition that victims would not be allowed to visit inmates in the system unless they went through a series of counseling sessions that were intended to prepare them for the visit. The inmate had a similar obligation. I also learned that the inmate had to acknowledge responsibility for the crime. Robert had not admitted any responsibility, and was in the midst of exercising his appeal rights. The door appeared to be closed.

I just happened to know someone in the upper management level of the prison system. I gave him a call and explained the circumstances. He promised to get back with me. As time went by, the chance of meeting with Robert seemed to dwindle. I kept praying.

Then, in March of 2011, I received a call from a prison official. My visit had been approved subject to a background check. Several days later I was informed that everything was in order. I was given a phone number to contact the person who would schedule the visit. It was set for April 21 from 1:30 to 2:30 in the afternoon.

In the meantime I had been contacted by Good Samaritan Ministries in Beaverton and asked to be the keynote speaker at their annual Good Friday luncheon on April 22, the day following my scheduled visit with Robert! The topic I was to speak on was ironically, forgiveness.

God's timing is absolutely perfect!

"For my thoughts are not your thoughts, neither are
your ways my ways, declares the Lord,

As the heavens are higher than the earth, so are my
ways higher than your ways and my thoughts than
your thoughts." Isaiah 55:8-9

The days flew by. I was praying that God would prepare my
heart and Robert's for this divine appointment. People would ask
me, "What is your plan?" or "What are you going to talk about?" or
"What are your expectations?" I told them that I didn't have a plan,
I didn't know what I was going to talk about and I didn't have any
expectations. I was just praying that God would prepare our hearts
for whatever He had in mind.

Five men from our Friday morning mens' group planned to go
with me to the Two Rivers Correctional Institution in Umatilla.
They were Randy Howarth, Brian Methvin, Jon Dobson, Lorne
Ray and Joe Dennis. It was a three-and-a-half hour trip. We all
rode together in a Suburban. On the way we shared stories of what
God was doing in our lives. One of the guys shared his powerful
testimony with us. We read scripture and we prayed.

We arrived at the prison at 1:00. Surrounding the prison was
a ten to twelve foot fence with razor wire attached to the top of it.
The prison houses about two thousand male inmates and was built
in 1999. It is considered a medium security prison.

I was scheduled to be there a half hour early to go through the
visitor processing center. I met the prison official who was in charge
of the Oregon prison visitor program. She guided me through the
processing center. From there, we went into the main prison area.
Several large, steel doors stood between us and the main housing
unit. As each door slammed behind me, the air became cold and
depressing. Darkness surrounded me as I realized the sobering truth
of what was about to take place.

As we walked down a hallway I noticed the main visitor area
through a windowed door. There were inmates in a large room the
size of a basketball gym. They were gathered around tables visiting
with relatives and friends.

The prison warden had reserved a small conference room for my visit with Robert. We walked into it and sat down. Shortly after we arrived, the warden came in to introduce himself. We talked briefly and he left.

There was a clock on the wall and it read 1:25.

My stomach turned. Five more minutes.

Our visit was scheduled from 1:30 to 2:30. I was in prison. Prison rules applied. One hour and one hour only. Another person entered the room. He was a high ranking prison guard who had been specifically assigned to us. He was a big guy. We agreed that he would sit behind Robert against the wall. I was on one side of a conference table and Robert would sit directly across from me. The visitor official sat next to me.

The door to the conference room was closed but there were some windows looking out into the hallway. Julie and I and scores of other people had been praying for weeks asking God to prepare our hearts, Robert's and the officials who were going to be in the room. I had no idea, NO IDEA, what was going to happen.

At about 1:30 I was told that Robert was on his way to the conference room. I glanced up and saw him through the window. Our eyes met, he put his head down, turned and walked away! I prayed to God that He would not let Robert abandon our meeting. We had come so close.

My prayer was quickly answered. Within a few seconds Robert returned, walking slowly into the room. I stood up, shook his hand and thanked him for agreeing to meet with me. We sat across from each other. He seemed nervous and uncomfortable. Me too.

I was very tense at this point, so I just started asking questions about his childhood, growing up, his mom and dad. As I began to run out of questions I looked at the clock. It read 1:35.

This was going to be a very long hour.

As I struggled to come up with more questions, I could tell Robert was also nervous. We spoke of our daughters. I asked how he met Megan. They met through a mutual friend. I asked about his daughter. She was now fifteen. She had visited him five times in the two years he had been in prison.

I was done. I had no more questions. It was 1:45. So I asked if he had any questions for me. He looked at me and the expression on his face began to change. He began to get tears in his eyes. He asked me, "How could you be so kind to me?"

I put my head in my hands. I began to cry and thanked God for opening the door to talk about what Jesus had done in my life. I said it wasn't me, but Jesus that was so kind. I told him that it was only through Jesus that I was able to endure the sorrow and grief over the loss of Megan. It was only through Jesus that I was able to forgive him. I told Robert again, as I told him at the trial, that I had forgiven him before I even knew who he was. I had no hatred, no bitterness and no anger. This could only happen because of Jesus.

The next forty-five minutes seemed like seconds as I explained how Jesus had transformed my life when I accepted Him as my Lord and Savior at the age of fifty-three. I shared how Jesus had taken a tragedy and turned it into triumph, had taken despair and turned it into hope and had taken sorrow and turned it into joy.

I gave Robert examples of how Jesus had used this tragedy to comfort other people in my role as a judge. I explained how God had given me opportunities to share the story of Megan and to pray with the victims of crime in my office. I was able to comfort people with the same comfort that I received from God.

At one point Robert looked at me and said softly, "I am so sorry." We weren't allowed to talk about the case, but I think I know what he meant.

I also told him that there were five guys in a Suburban in the parking lot praying for him at that moment. There were scores of others in the Portland area doing the same thing. I then asked him how I could pray for him. He wanted prayer for his daughter. I bowed my head and prayed out loud for his daughter and for him. I prayed for her protection, for her deliverance, for Robert's protection, for his deliverance and for Robert to know and feel the unconditional love and forgiveness of Jesus.

I know in my heart that Megan would have forgiven him also. She would have given Robert one of her business cards. She was a rescuer.

We talked for a few more minutes. It was 2:30. The prison guard escorted Robert out of the room. I was emotionally exhausted. The prison official was amazed at what just happened. A few minutes later the guard came back into the room. He said Robert had broken down in tears in the hallway and they had to wait until he regained his composure to be taken back into the general population. Inmates don't cry. The guard had never seen Robert cry. He was amazed.

The prison guard then told me that my words had been comforting to him. He had lost a son three years before in a shooting accident.

We never know who will be touched when we share how Jesus has worked in our life.

Jesus came crashing into the conference room at Two Rivers Correctional Institution on April 21, 2011. His forgiveness was and is life changing. As I finish this last paragraph, I have not yet heard from Robert. I know that Jesus is knocking on the door of his heart. Seeds have been planted.

"Here I am! I stand at the door and knock. If anyone hears my voice and opens the door, I will come in and eat with him, and he with me." Revelation 3:20

To The Reader

Thank you for traveling this journey with me. I hope that you will be able to share this book with someone you know who has gone through, or is in the midst of, a trial. We are all just one knock on the door from our knees.

I was so blessed that God did not permit unforgiveness to be part of this story. As a father, who lost a child to a brutal murder, I am still amazed that God did not allow hatred, anger or bitterness to germinate in my heart. As I said earlier in the book, there was no room for anything but sorrow and despair.

Looking back, it is still hard to imagine that I didn't have any thoughts of utterly causing gruesome acts of violence against Robert. It is a miracle.

One of the most sobering passages in the Bible is found at Matthew 6: 14-15 where Jesus said: "For if you forgive men when they sin against you, your heavenly Father will also forgive you. But if you do not forgive men their sins, your Father will not forgive your sins."

As much as God protected me during the loss of Megan, I have had numerous instances where I have been offended by people in the ordinary course of life. "Sinned against me!" I have held grudges. Much longer than I should have.

But if I don't forgive those who sin against me, then God won't forgive my sins. Scary. Sobering. Terrifying. Spine-chilling. But God...you don't know how bad they hurt me...how bad they hurt my feelings.

Forgiveness requires action. It takes a conscious effort to forgive. And it may require that action every day. How many times do you forgive? Take a look at Matthew 18:21-35:

> Then Peter came to Jesus and asked, "Lord, how many times shall I forgive my brother when he sins against me? Up to seven times?"
>
> Jesus answered, "I tell you, not seven times, but seventy-seven times."
>
> Therefore, the kingdom of heaven is like a king who wanted to settle accounts with his servants. As he began the settlement, a man who owed him ten thousand talents was brought to him. Since he was not able to pay, the master ordered that he and his wife and his children and all that he had be sold to repay the debt.
>
> The servant fell on his knees before him. "Be patient with me," he begged, "and I will pay back everything." The servant's master took pity on him, canceled the debt and let him go.
>
> But when that servant went out, he found one of his fellow servants who owed him a hundred denarii. He grabbed him and began to choke him. "Pay back what you owe me!" he demanded.
>
> His fellow servant fell to his knees and begged him, "Be patient with me, and I will pay you back."

But he refused. Instead, he went off and had the man thrown into prison until he could pay the debt. When the other servants saw what happened, they were greatly distressed and went and told their master everything that had happened.

Then the master called the servant in. "You wicked servant," he said, "I canceled all that debt of yours because you begged me to. Shouldn't you have had mercy on your fellow servant just as I had on you?" In anger his master turned him over to the jailers to be tortured, until he could pay back all he owed. This is how my heavenly Father will treat each of you unless you forgive your brother from your heart.

Unforgiveness is like being in prison. By failing to grant your offender forgiveness, you somehow think you are punishing them, sentencing them, holding them prisoner...when in reality, you are the one in prison. Everywhere you turn there are bars that are holding you back from joy, compassion, kindness...interfering with your ability to have relationships with others. And mostly interfering with your ability to talk to God, to commune with Him.

Don't you want to be released from that prison? Hasn't your sentence already been served by someone named Jesus? If you already haven't figured it out, you are the one that can unlock the door of your prison. You have the skeleton key. Put it in the keyhole and turn. Forgive. Not once, not twice, but seventy-seven times!

"If he sins against you seven times in a day, and seven times comes back to you and says, 'I repent,' forgive him." Luke 17:3-4

"Get rid of all bitterness, rage and anger, brawling and slander, along with every form of malice. Be kind and compassionate to one another, forgiving each other, just as Christ God forgave you." Ephesians 4:31-32

"As God's chosen people, holy and dearly loved, clothe yourselves with compassion, kindness, humility, gentleness and patience. Bear with each other and forgive whatever grievances you may have against one another. Forgive as the Lord forgave you. And over all these virtues put on love, which binds them all in perfect unity." Colossians 3: 12-14.

Is there someone in your life right now that you need to forgive? Do it. Turn the skeleton key and then throw it away. Step into the freedom of forgiveness!

Any thoughts? Contact me at twkohl@gmail.com

ACKNOWLEDGMENTS

I want to thank my wife and primary editor, Julie, for her endless patience and support as we have walked this journey together. Someone mentioned that the loss of a child to a couple results in divorce 85% of the time. For us, this journey has brought us even closer together.

I want to acknowledge and thank my son, Zac, for his strength, perseverance and forgiveness that he has shown throughout this trial.

I want to thank Phil Comer, the founding pastor of Solid Rock Church, who has been my friend and counselor for years. Solid Rock started out as a small church of about two hundred members, meeting in a middle school cafeteria and has grown to over six thousand in six short years. It gathers in three separate locations in the Portland metropolitan area.

Thanks to Bruce Heath for being my accountability partner since 2008.

I want to thank the men's group that meets every Friday morning at my house. Those men were, and are, a huge source of encouragement and support.

I want to thank Robert Hermann, the Washington County District Attorney, for supporting our drug court. Without Mr. Hermann's support, drug court could not have been established.

I want to thank Scott Healy, the Senior District Attorney in Clackamas County, Oregon, who was assigned to prosecute the murderer of my daughter. God picked the right person at the right time for the right job as He always does.

A special thanks to Melanie Dobson, who devoted countless hours to the final editing of this book, and to Joe Anfuso, Gerry Breshears, Cathy Dennis and Jay Fordice for their editorial comments.

There are numerous others who have prayed for and supported us during this time; many that I don't even know. I look forward to a glorious reunion in heaven and on the new earth with all of you.

And lastly, and most importantly, I want to thank God for the opportunity to share with others a story of hope, comfort and forgiveness that only He could author.

APPENDIX

Appendix A

You Never Let Go

Even though I walk through the valley of the shadow of death
Your perfect love is casting out fear;
And even when I'm caught in the middle of the storms of this life
I won't turn back, I know You are near.

> And I will fear no evil, for my God is with me
> And if my God is with me, whom shall I fear?
> Whom then shall I fear?
>
> Oh no, You never let go, through the calm and
> through the storm,
> Oh no, You never let go, in every high and every low
> Oh no, You never let go
> Lord, You never let go of me.

And I can see a light that is coming for the heart that holds on

A glorious light beyond all compare
And there will be an end to these troubles, but until that day comes
We'll live to know You here on the earth.

Yes, I can see a light that is coming for the heart
that holds on,
And there will be an end to these troubles, but until
that day comes,
Still I will praise You
Still I will praise You.
Written by Stephan Jenkin

APPENDIX B

Ten Key Components of Drug Courts

1. Drug courts integrate alcohol and other drug treatment services with justice system case processing.

2. Using a non-adversarial approach, prosecution and defense counsel promote public safety while protecting participants' due process rights.

3. Eligible participants are defined early and promptly placed in the drug court program.

4. Drug courts provide access to a continuum of alcohol, drug and other related treatment and rehabilitation services.

5. Abstinence is monitored by frequent alcohol and other drug testing.

6. A coordinated strategy governs drug court responses to participants' compliance.

7. Ongoing judicial interaction with each drug court participant is essential.

8. Monitoring and evaluation measure the achievement of program goals and gauge effectiveness.

9. Continuing interdisciplinary education promotes effective drug court planning, implementation and operations.

10. Forging partnerships among drug courts, public agencies and community-based organizations generates local support and enhances drug court.

APPENDIX C

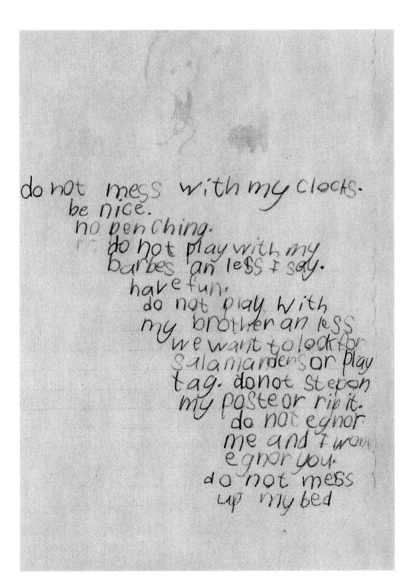

do not mess with my clocks.
be nice.
no penching.
do not play with my
barbes an less I say.
have fun.
do not play with
my brother an less
we want to look for
salamanders or play
tag. do not step on
my poste or rip it.
do not egnor
me and I wont
egnor you.
do not mess
up my bed

APPENDIX D

Dear Mom,

First, I'm sorry that I couldn't be there to share this moment with you...I want to tell you that I love you very much and am proud of you and the choices you have made in the last year. I remember when I was back home...and I sat with you during drug court. It was your turn to stand in front of the judge and he asked you if there was anything else you wanted to tell him and you said yes, that your daughter was here with you. I remember he asked me my name. I stood in front of Judge Kohl, told him my name and said if you went back to prison again I was done...Do you remember what he said? He said, "looks like you (mom) have a lot to lose, doesn't it?" You nodded your head, looked at me teary eyed and then looked at him and said, "yes Sir, I do."

I think that there are a lot of times that you think to yourself that you weren't a good mother, but you were and still are. Yes, obviously you've made some wrong choices in life, otherwise you wouldn't be standing in this courtroom right now, but haven't we all? The important thing is to learn from them and make your life better...

You have your OWN place, a very nice place at that, you went back to school last last year at the age of 52 and you've been clean and sober for almost a year and a half now with no relapses. All of these things I'm sure at one point or another you thought you couldn't do, but ARE doing. So, I want you to look at all these things you have accomplished in the last year and stand with your head high and finally be proud of yourself and continue to believe in yourself. I know, I'm sure Judge Kohl knows, the Drug Court team knows and I'm sure your fellow drug court members know that you are fully capable to continue down the path of sobriety and be successful the rest of your life...

I'm sure there are many people in the courtroom right now that will continue to be there for you, support you and encourage you, just like I will. Just remember you can do it, it may not be easy, because as we all know, nothing in life is ever easy, but you're strong and can get through it.

I do just have to say that just because you are graduating from drug court today, it doesn't mean that you're done with recovery. Recovery is a life long process that you will have to work on forever. Continue going to your meetings as often as you possibly can, because you and I both know what happens when you stop going and you don't want to have to face Judge Kohl again do you? Continue to surround yourself with others in recovery because they will hold you accountable and I expect them to hold you accountable. You've been in this program long enough to know that there are people everywhere watching you and looking out for you.

I owe a big thank you to Judge Kohl and the Drug Court team for not giving up on you and giving people with drug addictions a second, third or even a fourth chance to change their lives around and become productive members of society. Without you guys, I'm sure my mom would be sitting in prison...again.

Mom, congratulations on your graduation today and your continued sobriety. I don't think there are enough words to describe how extremely proud of you I am. Keep up the good work.

Love,

Your daughter

APPENDIX E

Dear Judge Kohl,

My name is Shannon, I am a grateful believer in Jesus Christ, and I struggle with chemical dependency, lust, lies, and criminality. I grew up in an alcohol and drug family. My parents divorced when I was 3, so I went back and forth between mom, dad, and my grandparents with lots of confusion. I remember going to church with my mom and when I would go to my fathers it would be a completely different lifestyle. It was very racial and filled with lots of hate. I remember getting beer for my father when I was 4 years old and taking drinks of it when I was bringing it to him. When I was 7, I was ran over by a 4-wheel drive truck. By the grace of God I'm still alive today. From that point I really believed in God and knew I was put on earth for a reason. My childhood was like a roller coaster. When I was 10, I started smoking pot. Then my mind of course changed and all the pain and struggle I was having began to go away. Also at the of 10, I was molested by a close family friend. I really didn't understand at the time I just felt in my heart it wasn't right. I didn't know how to tell anyone. I knew if I told my father the man would die. I knew if I told my mother she would tell my father and I didn't want to live my life without my father. So I tried to cover the pain up with pot. I was very shy from then on out. I wouldn't let people get close to me. I didn't trust anyone and the anger inside me got worse. The way I looked at people changed and not for the better. I was very spoiled and I got whatever I wanted. I went on to graduate high school and had a very good job coming out of high school. When I was 19 I got introduced to meth. I thought I saw a way to make a lot of money and very fast. I didn't like paying for it. I knew someone that made it. Then I got an idea. I would steal money from my father's bank account and would learn how to make it myself. That's when I really shut my life off from everyone, and I mean everyone. I isolated myself from the world and did what I thought would be the cure to all my pain. Little did I know I was going to destroy my life and everyone's around me. I really liked the money and my ego was very large. That lifestyle changed everything about me and after a while I started to realize all the lives I was destroying. In and out of jails, I really started to believe that was all I knew how to do. The only time I would talk to God was in jail. I would ask Him "Please Lord, get me through this one and I will get through the next one on my own." About 13 years of this going on, I started to really hate myself. Back to jail I go, sentenced to 6 months in the county. About 2 weeks goes by and I signed up to go to Church. I got on my knees and asked God to forgive me for my sins and invited him back into my life. Every time I got celled in, I would read my Bible. After doing this on a daily basis, I would begin to hear the Holy Spirit within me. I started to feel at peace and began to seek what I was put on earth to do. My sentence was up and I got out only going nowhere. Once again, I walked away from my Savior and I was back to doing the only thing I knew how to do. I tried to change, but I was scared of change and to learn something new like a better way to live. So, I tortured my life with the revolving door of jail for another year - this time leading me to a wonderful program called Drug Court. This is where I fully surrendered my will and my life over to God and started my journey with Celebrate Recovery on February of 2008. By doing so, God has given me the strength and courage to do His will, not my own. Thank you, Lord. This program has given me the tools and the treatment I had always needed and been there through everything. God has given me the spiritual kit I've needed to really work on myself and the things I thought I would never tell anyone about. He has also given me the power to forgive myself and the man I never thought I'd forgive. Since I've surrendered my life and my will over to my higher power, which is God, I have been able to work a 12 step program, and with each step I have learned a principal. When I worked the steps the first time, I wasn't completely honest with my fourth step, which is very vital to my recovery. I knew in my heart I wasn't honest and I caught myself falling backwards and getting very complacent. Also, it took a couple months to bring me out of it. It took me hearing someone else's story for me to realize I had to get rid of my secrets. I got into treatment so I could work on them and understood that it wasn't my fault and to forgive myself and the person that molested me. I knew I wasn't going to grow anymore so I asked my counselor if we could work on these things so I could keep moving forward in my recovery. Because I knew for sure I didn't want to go back to where I've been all my life. After working on myself and getting rid of that secret I was able to get completely honest about everything and start working the steps a second time by being completely honest, and start living by the principals. Today all I know how to do is the next right thing, to work on all my stuff and to grow spiritually in my recovery. Today I get to hit my knees every morning and pray to God and ask to do His will and not mine. By doing so, whatever I do that day is His will, I have a really good day. I get to help others and give back what has been freely given to me. By the changes in my life today I get asked to go places and speak my experience of strength and hope. I'm very proud of myself and as long as I stay teachable and in unity and keep the people I have around me today

I will be able to continue my journey in my recovery. This passage reminds me of my journey home to Christ:

> "For I know the plans I have for you," declares the Lord, "plans to prosper you and not to harm you, plans to give you hope and a future. Then you will call upon me and come and pray to me, and I will listen to you. You will seek me and find me when you seek me with all your heart."
> Jeremiah 29:11-13

As I continue on my journey of life, I just live by the principles of the program and most of all by God's will and not mine. Doing these very simple things, I've received many blessings. The relationship with my 12 year old son that I had no contact with for over six years is so awesome; it is like I had never been gone from his life. Thank you, Jesus! I have been a productive member of society and been able to fulfill my lifelong dream of being a firefighter. I can look myself and everyone else in the eyes with no worries. Life is what you make it for a recovering addict; having God and recovery in your life makes all things possible. I know for me I have to live this life each and every day for the rest of my life. I just want the whole world to know that no matter what age you are, it's not too late to change your life.

Shannon

APPENDIX F

Honorable Thomas Kohl,

I hope this letter finds you well. I have seen better days but I cannot complain. Today was an eye opening day for me. I am writing to you because I owe it to you and the series that I saw your story on, "From Drugs to Mugs".

I am terribly sorry for your loss. I want to tell you that I haven't cried in so many years, until today. It is very hard to explain what happened. I don't understand how and why but I would like to try...

I am 32 years old and I have been in jail or prison or on parole since I was 17. I am amazed that I never realized (or admitted) in all these years that I am a drug addict. I finally started thinking about it a few days ago, after a series of conversations I had with my girlfriend, who is and always has been drug free. I gave my past a serious look and decided to take a class here at the Calhoun County Jail called "Ladder to Recovery". Today we watched the first of seven parts, "From Drugs to Mugs".

I was _floored!_ So much of what was said relates to me. Then the story of your daughter. Oh my God, I am so very sorry, your Honor. My heart is crushed....

I am so embarrassed and ashamed of the things I have done. I feel so stupid for taking so long to admit that I am a drug addict.

My problem is prescription pills. Mainly Vicodin. I started out taking them for my injuries in an accident. At the time of my arrest I was taking 30 to 40 Narco/Vicodin a day! I would do anything for the drug. It is so stupid. I was going to the local college here in Battle Creek, Michigan for computer engineering and earning nearly a 4.0 and at night I was involving myself in stolen property to get drugs.

I don't know if I can fix my life. I don't know how! I have the desire but I am unsure of what to do! I have children and I am ruining their lives by being a drug addict. The programs offered in the Michigan Dept. of Corrections only require that you pull up a chair. There may be programs offered at the county jail level, I am unsure of even how to find out. I am lost and confused but I want to live a different life but I honestly don't know if I can without guidance.

I am in awe of you and that you offer a "drug court" after what happened with your beautiful little girl. But, what you are doing is the right thing and so honorable and REAL that it has touched my heart.

I know that you are a good man and probably a great judge. I hope that the drug court that you offer helps many people. I only wish for the opportunity to participate in a program such as that.

I never really had a family. My father was only there to beat on us. We often went without meals. I went to prison at 17 years old and have been back and forth since. I never stole or hurt (physically) from my family, but didn't get a single visit from them. That was really hard for me, especially at 17 years old.

I have never had a friend in my life until my girlfriend. Her family is what a family should be. She is there for me. She tells me when I am wrong. I had to learn, I am still learning, how to live an "adult life" because I have never been on my own. When my family recognized my drug addiction, they used it to get me to break laws for them. My girlfriend warned me, but I didn't listen.

As I gain knowledge of all these things, and also face the reality that I may not get the help I need, I start to wonder about if, and when, our courts in Michigan will start to use rehabilitation. I have NEVER had the chance.

I want you to know, Mr. Kohl, you have already made the world a better place and the courts all over the United States need men like yourself. I admire you and I have never met you. You are what we need. You represent the change our society needs. You have touched my heart from the other side of our country. Please don't ever give up. We need you!

Cordially and with Honor and Respect,

E.P.

/

CPSIA information can be obtained at www.ICGtesting.com
Printed in the USA
BVOW002359120513

320438BV00003B/4/P